Finally!

Becoming Who You Were Always Meant to Be

PEGGY ROMERO

FINALLY!

Interior and Cover Design by
Transcendent Publishing
PO Box 66202
St. Pete Beach, FL 33707
www.transcendentpublishing.com

Paperback ISBN: 979-8-9865751-0-0

Hardcover ISBN: 979-8-9865751-1-7

Disclaimer: I have tried to recreate events, locales and conversations from my memories of them. To maintain their anonymity, in some instances I have changed the names of individuals and places.

Printed in the United States of America.

This book is dedicated to my three beautiful children, Melissa, Tyler, and Kimberly. During their young lives they endured many struggles and challenges, none of their own making, and never failed to meet them with a strength, resiliency, and capacity for joy that amazes me to this day. Through all the good and the bad, the changes and the moves, they have been my rocks and my dearest loves. I am honored to be their mother.

TABLE OF CONTENTS

FOREWORD

My life has been a journey that has taken me around the world and given me the opportunity to meet some talented and special people. These individuals inspired me through their stories of perseverance, overcoming all odds, to create a life of success and influence. When I met Peggy Romero and heard her story, I was captivated and truly amazed at what she had accomplished.

I met Peggy through her sister Jennifer, with whom I had worked with in the past. Peggy was looking to hire a coach, but her sister warned me that she was very stubborn and not sure if she could work with me. I interviewed Peggy to see if she and I would be a good synergetic fit for Shift Coaching. I had heard so much about this woman and her accomplishments, I was excited for this meeting. She was tough, no nonsense, and dare I say pretty stubborn, as she told me how I should coach her and what she would and would not do. I could see through this tough exterior that there was something deep within her that needed to be expressed. What came out is the book you are reading today, *Finally! Becoming Who You Were Always Meant to Be.*

Peggy's story seems so improbable that it seems like a Hollywood script. In *Part One: Becoming Who They Told Me to Be,* Peggy shares her story of hardships, challenges, and how she defied the odds. Peggy was raised to be a submissive housewife catering to a husband and raising a family. The messages she received as a child were not to dream and fit in her domestic role. Yet, for Peggy, this wasn't her true-self, which would reveal itself through hardship, trials, and overcoming all obstacles. The one thing the reader will see as they read this first part of the book. That even though Peggy was stuck in abusive situations, she had true faith that she was one of God's chosen ones.

Peggy's story will take you on a ride that would have destroyed many. She made the impossible possible through unprecedented courage to move through diversity and start over when needed, but never quit. She raised three children by herself, built businesses through trial and error, got a college degree at age forty-five, and became a self-made success story. If anyone looked at the life she was born into, they would declare these results "IMPOSSIBLE."

In *Part Two – Becoming Who I Was Born to Be*, Peggy reveals her secrets to success and her true mission, which drove her through such adversity to success. Her mission was to set a legacy for her three children, so they could live their dreams and not have to endure the hardships she lived through. Peggy built a life that allowed her sisters to see what was truly possible following her success, and a life that allows her children to dream that they can do whatever they desire. In *Chapter Ten: Find Your Why*, Peggy gives you the blueprint needed for you, the reader, to connect and find your story to build your own legacy.

I have had the honor of working with Peggy for several years, and I am confident when I say this is an incredible woman and a story that has inspired me personally. Having daughters and now a granddaughter, I believe Peggy's story shows what is possible for today's women, even though many times the odds are stacked against them. It is of the utmost honor to write this foreword for a woman I respect and admire. *Finally!* is one of those books that will inspire many now and for the generations still to come. I personally look forward to the day they make this book into a movie.

Bill Cortright, International Best-Selling Author and Creator of Stress Mastery

INTRODUCTION

*E*veryone is afraid sometimes. In fact, fear is not only a normal part of life but a mechanism designed to protect us from danger. Living in fear, however, is something entirely different. It keeps us small and prevents us from stepping into our full potential. If you are reading this book, you, like so many others out there, may feel that you are not living the life you were meant to live, as the strong, capable person you know dwells inside you. Why is this? While the details will be different for each of us, I would wager that they are all rooted in the fears we carry.

Have you ever thought about your fears? I mean, really took the time to consider them? (Hint: they are not always on the surface, but can be years or even decades old and buried in the hidden recesses of our minds.) Let's ask the question another way – what do you wish you had the courage to do? When you think of these dreams and aspirations, what kinds of thoughts pop into your head to convince you they're not possible? That, my friends, is the voice of fear.

Fear stops us from doing things we want to do and from saying things we want to say. Again, some fears are healthy – they may even stem from our intuition trying to keep us out of harm's way.

However, many (or even most) of our fears are the irrational kind. They are illusions, created by negative thought loops and "what-if" scenarios. It is only when we can recognize them and learn to let them go that we set ourselves free and open space for our lives to drastically change for the better.

You're probably asking, "How do I release my fears, especially those I don't even know are there?" The first step is to look within, take an inventory, and really get to know yourself, possibly for the first time in your life. This is not a quick fix, but a journey that requires patience and compassion as those hidden fears are inevitably triggered by life circumstances. Even the ways those triggers show up are different for us. My reaction to fear, and the stress it causes, is to become violently sick to my stomach, be it pain or vomiting. Now, instead of being debilitated by it or mindlessly powering through, I recognize it as an opportunity to examine what is really happening inside and deal with it.

It's never easy to look inside ourselves, to make change. We will stay in marriages because we fear the unknown. We'll keep a job because we are afraid of what the next job will bring. We hang out with friends and family who are not good for or to us, because we are afraid we won't be loved. We hide who we really want to be because we are afraid people will judge us. We don't allow ourselves to dream because of fear of failure, or the fear that we will succeed and no longer fit in with our tribe. We do everything to avoid rattling the cage, *even as we long to escape it.*

If you continue the same way, you will keep missing out on the magnificent life God intended you to have.

Once upon a time (and for a long time), this was my story. In fact, for much of my life I was so scared I could barely breathe, never mind make a move. My family was built on a paradigm of fear – I was taught to always play safe and to play small. By the time I was sixteen, I had quit dreaming of a career for myself and started praying for a husband to love me. Yes, I still secretly wanted more, but I held it in my heart, embarrassed and afraid to tell anyone.

Most of us can point to some event or circumstance that forced our hand and made us step out of our comfort zone. For me, that was my children. As a young, divorced mother, I no longer had the option of accepting jobs that barely put food on the table. My parents had seven kids. They weren't good with money and we never had enough. We had to share everything – not just toys, but our clothes and even our socks! I hated it, and I vowed my own children would have a different kind of life. They would have their own shoes, coats, and lots of clothes. They would get an allowance so they could have fun on the weekends, and if they chose, be able to go to college. Most importantly, I vowed I would listen to their dreams and do everything in my power to help make them a reality.

But how to do this? How would I start from the bottom? What was my first move? Yes, I was fearful – I had every kind of fear imaginable – but lying there full of shame was not an option. This was when I first began to tell myself things like:

Do it scared, but do it anyway.
You can't ever give up.
You are better than they say you are.

As I moved forward for my children, I began rediscovering my own long-lost dreams and aspirations – and unravelling the fears that had kept me from reaching for them. It was an often uncomfortable and painful process with plenty of trials and errors, but it has also led to incredible joy, success, and growth.

In the pages that follow, you will understand why I like to say that I was born on February 11, 1989, at the age of twenty-seven. I will share with you my story, from helping to parent my siblings at a young age to stretching every dollar to raise my own children; from living in a tiny apartment to buying my first home and creating several businesses. It all happened because I took a breath and, with my heart pounding out of my chest with fear, took a leap and kept moving. It will also, hopefully, fulfill another dream of mine: to help empower others like you to do the same.

So you also get to say, "Today I face my fear and do it anyway. Today is my birthdate!"

Part One

Becoming
Who They Told Me to Be

Chapter One

MY BEGINNINGS

As you read my story, it may be hard to imagine, but for as long as I can remember I have known right from wrong. My parents intended to raise me and my six siblings to be good people. Follow the rules, respect your elders and obey the Ten Commandments. But there was a disconnect between saying and doing – a pretense, if you will. "Don't do as I do, do as I say" was one of my dad's sayings. And, if it was going to benefit her, my mom said things like, "Just do it, you can go to confession later" or "God wouldn't have given you the opportunity if He didn't want you to take it," which I interpreted as you can do whatever you wanted all week as long as you went to church on Sunday and asked Him for forgiveness. On the other hand, we were continually told we'd go to hell for this offense or that sin. Other dire consequences including being punished by God in this life for undesirable behavior, and "If you make faces your face will freeze like that." I am not sure whether she actually believed the things she told us or if they were just tools she used to try to keep her large, unruly brood in order.

My Parents

Dad was born in 1934 to Mexican immigrants on an Indian Reservation in New Mexico. I honestly don't know if my grandparents, Albert and Grace, were legal citizens or not, but I do know that they were both of Spanish heritage and had been born, raised, and married in Mexico. After living in New Mexico for a time they moved to Oregon to raise their family. My dad, the second-oldest of their four kids, was an extremely hard worker. When he was in high school he lied about his age to join the Airforce, where he spent the next four years and served in the Korean War. He was married to my mother by the time he was twenty-five.

Mom, who was born in 1936, was also the child of immigrants in search of the American Dream. Agnes and Willie were both born in Ireland and came to the United States separately, both willing to work hard to make it in their adopted country. They met in New York City, married, and had eleven children; my mom was fourth from the youngest. The oldest were twins, Helen and Agnes, the latter of whom – to the delight of her family – became a nun. Helen met and married a merchant marine who had been at port in New York for just two weeks. He went back out for another year to complete his duty, and she took a train out to Oregon to live with her new husband's family because "That's what you do." A visit to Aunt Helen turned out to be a life-changer for my mom; she met my father, whose parents lived next door, and they fell in love. Four months later they were married; the date, January 31, 1959. Nine months later, my brother was born. Life was such a whirlwind that Mom didn't go back to New York for four or five years.

My parents went on to have seven children and stayed married until the day my dad died at the untimely age of sixty-two. Mom, who survived him by twenty years, never even considered marrying again.

The reason I am sharing all of this history is so you can see and understand that I come from a line of hard-workers and risk-takers, who despite fears and obstacles were willing to do whatever it took to build a better life. What guts my Irish grandmother – whose real name was Bridget – must have had to leave her family behind and get on that enormous ship headed for an unfamiliar land! Arriving in New York with a little money she had saved and just a few changes of clothes, she settled, like so many other immigrants, in a crowded tenement house. Bridget soon learned that many of her new countryman hated the Irish, labeling them "lazy drunks" and often refusing to hire them. Hoping to get a job and some respect, she decided to change her name to Agnes, which sounded "less Irish." Her only friend in those early days was a cousin she had written to before leaving Ireland. My grandmother was just twenty years old.

My grandparents endured hardships in the 1920s that are unimaginable to most Americans today. I haven't always been nearly as strong, but it is a comfort to know that their grit and determination to "just do it" courses through my veins, and of this I am very proud.

Formative Years

I remember being four years old and waiting for my brother Chris to come home from school on a yellow school bus. I was small, and even stepping on my tippy toes I could barely manage to peer through the glass window of our old farmhouse. I dearly loved Chris, who was a year and a half older, and missed him when he was gone. We had a great big front yard and a long driveway, and I scanned them both, anxiously anticipating the first glimpse of him as he walked to the house. When after what seemed like forever, he finally appeared, I would rush to the door to meet him, then follow him to the kitchen to wait for Mom to get us a snack. Many afternoons we enjoyed tea and toast as Mom and I happily listened to Chris tell us about his time at school and all he'd learned that day. Every night our parents would come to each of our rooms and pray with us: "God bless Mommy and Daddy and all my brothers and sisters, and Baby Jesus keep us safe. Amen."

One day, I think Chris was at school at the time, I was under the kitchen table, trying to keep myself occupied until he came home. My parents were talking just a few feet away and Mom was ironing Dad's shirts. She was also crying. They couldn't see me, because there was a tablecloth hanging down and I stayed very quiet; I knew I shouldn't be hearing this conversation, realizing, even at this young age, that it was sacred, just between them. I didn't understand it, but there was something about my dad leaving, like moving to a different home; there was mention of some other woman. I'm not sure what happened after that, but I don't think he left, not even for one night. I loved my dad and I didn't know who the lady was, but I didn't want him to go live with her. Life was good for me, but I guess maybe not too good for them.

We lived on five acres in the country. Dad went to work every day and Mom stayed home and took care of all of us. Mom was great at running the household. She canned vegetables from the garden and made jam from fruit plucked right from trees on our property. The house was always clean and dinner was always on the table when Dad got home. And somehow she still found the time to get dressed up – she wore dresses almost every day, usually with an apron over them, and her hair was always done.

Living out in the big house in the country was fun – there was always plenty of things to do. In the summer we had a big garden, and we would help Mom pick the berries and dig up the potatoes. I also remember having lots of tomatoes, corn, apples, cherries and peaches. Mom made applesauce, jelly and apple crisp. My dad loved peaches. I'd gladly climb the trees to get the fruit for him or anyone else who wanted it. I was a tomboy through and through. I loved it out there on the property.

When it was cold or rainy outside, I could usually be found in the playroom in the attic. There was a really great kitchen in there and I loved to cook and serve meals to the other kids. There was water that ran into the sink, as long as you put some in the container underneath. I had dishes and everything. I even had fun cleaning up.

Our neighbors had horses and gave us rides sometimes. They had woods behind their house with lots of trails and they rode fast through those trails while I held on for dear life. It was so fun and exciting, but scary. I loved it and wanted to have a horse of my own someday. Our mailboxes were at the end of that long driveway and they'd give one of us a ride there sometimes. I kept asking to ride a horse myself and finally they let me – never alone, though; they walked alongside me. One day, I fell off a horse, and though I don't think I was really hurt, I was very scared. I was told that I had to get right back up on that horse, that day. I did, but I never asked to learn to ride alone again. In fact, I'm not even sure I went horseback riding with them after that.

We had a neighbor named Charlie Brown and he and his wife used to let me and my siblings visit them. But only two of us were allowed at a time, and only after they'd had breakfast. We used to go to the end of the road to get the newspaper and bring it to them. They too lived on five acres, maybe ten, and had cows and chickens and a big garden to tend to. No wonder they didn't want us to come too early!

We had lots of visitors at our house as well. Mom's cousins lived in the convent, and they came to our house and played baseball and tag with us. Dad's parents came over regularly, and his brother and sisters too. After so many years in this country my grandparents were Americanized and always spoke to us in English. They still spoke Spanish in their own home, though, and once in a while they'd say something to each other in Spanish, like a secret. I wanted to know what they were saying, and had fun guessing.

I was the only female grandchild they had for a long time and I would get to go spend the night with my gramma. She was a very gentle woman, soft spoken, and she always made me feel so special. I learned that she had passed away while I was on the train returning from a visit to Mom's family in New York. She had gone to heaven, Mom said. I was only about seven years old but I understood what that meant. I knew I'd never see her again and I was already missing her.

Chris

We had a big barn that had a wall full of kennels, lots of them. We didn't use them for anything; they were just there when we moved in. Many of them had stuff in them – things like leather strips, cotton, not sure what else. There were two big rooms in the barn and a big hayloft on one side that had a homemade ladder leading up to it. It was so fun to go up there! We could play for hours; we had great imaginations and plenty of energy. We never ran out of places to explore. One day, we were in the barn and heard the sound of "mew, mew" coming from one of the kennels. When we investigated, we found a litter of kittens, so sweet, so soft and cuddly. We were told not to mess with them; they were babies and needed to be taken care of by their mother. I remember Chris putting one of them in a bag and swinging the bag around and around over his head and throwing it into the field. I begged him to be nice. He never listened to me. He did it a few times then he did it without the bag. He swung them around by the tail and threw it as far as he could. He was so mean to those cats and I never knew why or how he could be so cruel.

Looking back, I realize this was a sign of things to come with Chris. As much as I loved my brother, I knew at a very young age that he didn't have the same heart as I did. Early on I made a decision to be good and try my best not to do bad things; Chris was the opposite. It was in that barn that he got all of us to dance naked. We were just little kids, babies even. He was probably only seven or eight, so how did he even come up with ideas like that? I don't know why he wanted to do it. I may have done it once, but knew it was wrong. I did my best to stop the other littler kids from doing things that were wrong, but Chris was relentless.

One time he stole my mom's cigarettes and took us to a neighbor's property and got us all to smoke with him. I hadn't even started first grade yet; the other boys were not more than three and four. I still remember the time we were under a tree, past the big garden across the field and under a barbed wire fence. All of a sudden, here comes Mom, walking across that big field, carrying a piece of hot wheels track. Boy, were we in trouble! She chased us all back to the house and told us we were to stay in our rooms. I never stole her cigarettes again. I was sorry... *really* sorry.

It was also at that house that the boys came up with their imaginary friend, Charny, and introduced us to him. Charny, who was about five years old, would play all the games with us, but then he started doing mean things. Like one time, I saw my little sister Jenny drinking muddy water, which the boys had given her and said it was iced tea. When I went over to put a stop to it, they told me it was Charny who had given it to her. I said Charny wouldn't do that because Charney was good, but Chris explained that there was a "Bad Charny" too. Chris was always looking for trouble, and trying to get the younger kids to follow his lead, while I tried to get them to ignore him.

Despite my efforts, I think my brother's behavior shaped my life and the lives of our five siblings. Chris demanded eighty percent of my parents' time, leaving twenty percent for the rest of us. He also succeeded getting ahold of the boys, and I spent much of my time keeping my sisters away so they wouldn't get into trouble too.

Confession

By the time I was in second grade we had left the barn, the woods, Charlie Brown, and the horses behind and moved to Portland. I went to Catholic school and had a blue plaid uniform. I loved it. I was a good student and was happy with the nuns who ran the school. Nuns and priests were also a big part of our homelife. Several of my mother's relatives were nuns, and Mom and Dad had friends who were priests, including Father Kevin, the principal of the school.

He came to our house for dinner many Sunday afternoons after church. Whenever we had visitors, my siblings and I were allowed to stay for an hour before being shooed from the room; "Go play," we were told. Always afraid of missing something, I'd try to sneak back and hear what they were talking about. I also remember at one point wanting to be a nun myself. My parents would have been very happy with that decision!

Second grade was a big year for me. I was going to make my First Communion. Each morning I headed to school early so I could attend mass before classes started. My brothers didn't want to go to daily mass, so I walked alone. One morning, one of my classmates, Kevin LaRue, took communion. I was appalled! Catholic children received the sacraments – baptism, First Confession, and First Communion in that order. When I called Kevin out on it (as if it were any of my business), he told me he had made his communion the previous year. This turned into a several rounds of "Did not!"; "Did to!" until I gave up the argument and lied, telling him I had made my communion as well.

The next morning, I went up and took communion. Oh my gosh, I felt so guilty, thinking, *Oh, God please forgive me.* I didn't take it anymore after that, and when Kevin asked me why I told him I just didn't feel like it. The story doesn't end there. Later in the year, we were to receive the Sacrament of Confession so that we could start to receive our First Communion. I had been dreading this day for months. I would have to bare my soul, confess my sin of taking communion that day before I was supposed to. On the other hand, I was truly excited by the idea that I'd be pure as snow as soon as I admitted what I'd done. I was looking forward to getting it off my chest. Usually, when you go to confession you are in a little booth. There is a curtain between you and the priest you are confessing to, and in my young mind I figured that since he couldn't see me he wouldn't know who I was. Maybe I could even try to disguise my voice to throw him off. Imagine my horror when I learned our confession was to be face-to-face with Father Kevin!

I walked toward him with fear and reverence, knowing this was a no-win situation. If I didn't confess taking communion that day, I would go to hell. If I told him the truth, I would be completely embarrassed by what a bad kid I was. How would I ever move on from this? Would Father Kevin tell my parents? Would he still like me? Finally, I decided to just bite the bullet and tell the truth. I was NOT going to hell over this, not if I could save myself now.

"Forgive me, Father, for I have sinned; this is my first confession..." Then I took a deep breath and, with tears in my eyes, started rambling. "I took communion, but only once, and not only that, I was jealous! Jealous of Kevin LaRue. I am so sorry. I never did it again. I don't want to go to hell"

Father Kevin looked at me with his beautiful gentle smile and asked, "Anything else?"

Anything else? What could be worse than that? What kind of kid did he think I was?

"Well, I don't always obey my mother..."

He then delivered my penance: "Say ten Our Fathers and ten Hail Marys."

"Are you going to tell my parents?" I blurted out, in fear of the impending punishment that may be coming.

"No, Peggy, what you say in confession is confidential."

Music to my ears! "But, do you forgive me?"

"Yes, of course, and God does too. Don't worry about it again."

That day I knew for sure that God is great! I was as free as a bird. I happily said my penance and was never scared about the wrath of God again. Forgiveness is awesome!

Chosen

This part of my story has been monumental in my life. It was also a little crazy, maybe even hard to believe, but it's absolutely true. At seven years old, I had an experience that many people dream about but don't ever have.

One day after school I was down in the church basement, waiting for my baton lessons to start. There was a lot of commotion, with little girls in uniforms running around and the nuns trying to get us settled. There was a large space in the front where the instructor could stand to show us what to do, and two sections of seats, with five or six rows in each section and about six chairs in each row. I was sitting in the far-left chair of the front row in the section on the left. Nobody else had sat down in my row yet.

Suddenly, it was as if Jesus Himself came and sat next to me. It was as if He had His arm around me. It was as if He *knew* me. He knew my name and everything about me. He loved me. I knew that God Himself came to me that day and without an audible word, said *Peggy, you are special to me; I love you; I will always be with you. You don't need to be afraid; I am always here for you.*

My heart filled with love. I felt like I was God's favorite.

Now, when that happens to you, you don't ever forget it. Nobody can talk you out of it or make you think you may have misunderstood or been confused, though they may certainly try.

When I tried to tell a few people about my visit with Jesus, they did not take me seriously – one of the nuns even said it was blasphemy! – so I kept it to myself for decades. I didn't want to go to hell. I also didn't want anyone else to feel bad about the fact that I was God's favorite, or think I was crazy because I believed it. But to this day *I know that I know that I know* what happened in that church basement was real. There can be no misunderstanding or confusion about it.

It would be several years later, at Vacation Bible School through a Baptist church, when I came to understand it is okay to have a personal relationship with Jesus. I am still not sure why I was chosen to hear from God, but as that relationship grew stronger I realized the truth: that YOU are God's favorite too.

When I was in the fourth grade, Father Kevin got sick. I wanted to see him, but my parents said he wasn't up to it and they would let me know when he could have visitors. Unfortunately, that never happened; he had a brain tumor and it turned out to be fatal. They had him laid out at church and the whole school walked by him. It was the first time I had seen a dead body. I still remember what he looked like and the big scar on his head. I assume that was from surgery. Not sure why I had to see that, but I did.

A new priest took Father Kevin's place at church, and for some reason the school closed down. I went to public school after that, but for a while I held onto my dream of becoming a nun. I still walked to mass before school, then would go back home to change out of one of the two dresses I owned before heading out the door again to Vestal Elementary School. At first I wasn't sure I'd like it, but eventually it got better. I made friends with the kids there, and I loved my gym teacher, Mr. Roy. He was so good to me and openly admitted to everyone that I was his pet. I was the line leader, the exercise demonstrator and team captain. I'm not sure why he liked me so much – there was never anything weird or inappropriate about it – but to this day Mr. Roy is one of my fondest memories of that school.

Of course it wasn't all a bed of roses. That first year at Vestal, I broke my arm. A girl named Karol was pushing me on the rings.

"Stop, stop," I said, but I was laughing, and Poor Karol had no idea that I was losing my grip.

For the first few minutes after I fell it didn't hurt – maybe because I was in shock – but I'm sure I cried when I saw it. You could tell it was broken – it went in a "V" between my wrist and my elbow. The school called an ambulance, and I got my arm set and spent the night at the hospital. It turned out to be not that bad – Aunt Helen, the world's greatest aunt, bought me a David Cassidy album, and I loved all the attention. All the kids signed my cast, as did Mr. Roy. I had no idea what "Lindsey 10/12/72" meant, and it would be at least five years before I learned that Lindsey was his first name.

While I still had the cast on my arm I was playing with my brother and ended up banging my head on the coffee table. It was back to the hospital for stitches, but that injury didn't hurt either. I was a tomboy, and I was tough.

In the fifth grade I planned a surprise birthday party for my teacher, Ms. Daugherty. I baked cupcakes at home and brought them to school. December 6 – I can still remember the date. Mr. Roy helped us get her out of the room for a minute while we set up the cupcakes and punch. She was so happy and very surprised when she came back into her party. We had made her a card too, and the whole class signed it. It was great!

That same year they started bussing black kids from the other side of town to our all-white school – part of an effort to end segregation. I made fast friends with a girl named Otie; I thought it was the coolest thing ever that she had her ears pierced, and a little piece of a toothpick in there instead of earrings!

I remember being so excited when Otie and I planned a sleepover – my first with a friend from school. When the big day, a Friday, arrived, Otie came home with me after school. We were out playing when my dad got home. Next thing you knew, we were driving her home.

"Why, Dad, why?" I asked, completely confused. After all, our mothers had said yes to the sleepover!

I don't remember what he told me when the three of us were in the car; however, after we dropped Otie off he told me that we didn't live in a place where negros (the word people used at the time) were accepted. I could be friends with Otie at school but bringing her home would "cause trouble." Of course, I had no idea about these rules, and I would learn a hard lesson that day. Prejudice, though it had no rhyme or reason, could actually prevent me from being around people I cared about. I didn't understand it then and I never will. I just hoped, and still do, that Otie never knew why she had to go home early.

The Big Move

I didn't go to that school for long either. My mom's sister and her family came out from New York to visit us and we had such a blast with them that I guess Mom got homesick. All of a sudden, we were leaving our fantastic home and all our friends and moving across the country. I had no idea why it was so urgent for us to leave right then, and at twelve years old I was not getting any kind of explanation. It just didn't make sense. My dad had a great job and we were living in a great neighborhood. Life was good, or so it seemed to me.

I do remember, though, that just a month or so before our quick departure, Chris had used lighter fluid to set a kid's coat on fire. He doused the fur lining, probably not flame-retardant back in the early seventies, and got a fire going... in the kid's hood! I was not there when it happened, but I was hiding behind the piano and listening to the police tell my mom what Chris had done. This came after Chris's non-stop torment of the kid, whose name was Steve, for weeks, if not months. When poor Steve committed suicide not long after the incident, I blamed my brother. He was so cruel and seemingly remorseless, and Steve probably couldn't stand the pain of his harassment anymore. I hope that's not true, but the fact is the fire probably pushed him over the edge. *Thanks a lot, Chris. Because of you we're now moving to New York.*

Looking back, though, I can also see that Mom really did want to be near her family again, and who could blame her? She had come to Oregon for a two-week visit and wound up staying fifteen years. Then again, I've always imagined that we moved because my dad was out too much, leaving my mother home with us kids. Not sure if there was a lot more to it or not. I know there were times when we got up for the day before my dad returned from partying the night before. And, I had never forgotten the talk of the other woman and assumed that kind of thing was always going on at that time. Honestly, I have no way of knowing if it happened or why he couldn't be faithful to my poor mom, but that really had to hurt.

Chapter Two

THE GOOD GIRL

When we first got to New York we stayed with relatives in Rockland County, about a forty-minute drive from Manhattan. There were so many of us that we split up – Mom, sisters and I lived with Aunt Nan and Uncle Danny, and my dad and the boys were across town at another aunt's house. Aunt Nan and Uncle Danny had seven kids of their own, five of them still at home, so I have no idea how we piled in on top of them. My most pleasant memories of that time were of my cousin, Kevin. He was like the big brother I wish I had – always kind, always showing me love. His attention changed me somehow; it created confidence and a feeling of worthiness. It helped shape the person I am today, for which I am forever grateful. My time with him was over too soon.

I can't explain how hard it was to find my way that year. I felt so disconnected, so lost and vulnerable. It made it worse that we moved after the school year started. I used to go check on my younger siblings and talk to the teachers who would allow it. My brother's teacher, Mr. McConnel, gave me the biggest compliment

I'd ever had when he wrote in my autograph book, "A visitor from afar who blessed our hallways with her presence and smiles."

What? He noticed me. He thinks I am a blessing? It's hard to explain, but that girl that he saw, that is who I have always wanted to be. Sometimes you just don't know how your words affect another person. I felt so special when I read that note, and it continues to bless me every time it comes to mind.

Our move East brought another enormous change: my mother began working outside the home. The good-paying job Dad thought he was going to get with the sheet metal union didn't work out, and the one he got didn't pay nearly enough. Suddenly we were poor – really poor – as in, not much food and no extra anything. For Christmas that year I asked for a candle-making kit. It was five dollars. I didn't get it. I don't remember what the boys got. Nancy and Jenny each got a Barbie and Kelly got a baby doll. I got an outfit. Plaid pants and a bodysuit; the cuffs and collar were the same plaid as the pants. It was okay and I'm sure I needed it, but I really wanted the candle-maker. We were used to getting several gifts each, more than we even asked for.

I didn't like this new place at all.

Dad worked in Manhattan and wasn't home much during the week. To bring in more money he got a swing shift position in addition to his day job, so he slept in his car in the city so he could save the time, tolls and the gas driving back and forth. The tolls were expensive, plus the commute would cut into his sleep time. Mom was waitressing in the evenings and weekends, so we were alone most of the time, our parents no longer there with us, or for us. Chris didn't help, which left me in charge of the younger kids.

My life had changed so dramatically and abruptly. There I was, in the sixth grade with five children to take care of – a job I was ill-equipped to handle. One day two of my little sisters, Kelly and Jenny, came home crying. They had been walking over by the store and through a snow-covered vacant lot and Kelly fell. When I saw Kelly's arm I nearly passed out. The skin and fat and everything inside were now on the outside. I could see the bone! I wrapped it in a kitchen towel and called my aunt, who came and took her to the hospital while I stayed with the other kids. The whole time, my thoughts were racing like a freight train. *I am going to be in so much trouble. I can't believe I let this happen! I failed; I wasn't responsible. I wanted to go to the hospital with them so bad but they made me stay behind.* I was scared and hurt and angry all at the same time.

I quickly shifted the blame to poor Jenny, who was the older of the two.

"You shouldn't have gone that way," I told her. "If she dies, it's your fault. You shouldn't have taken the shortcut. You're not allowed to go over there." Yes, I said that to a seven-year-old. But in my defense, I was only twelve myself and shouldering a tremendous responsibility that I wasn't ready for. It always rolls downhill, right? Luckily for me and my sisters, Kelly had sustained nothing more than a nasty cut that required stitches inside and out. Otherwise, she was okay, thank you, God.

Another time, Chris and I were making french fries. We heated up a pot full of grease while we peeled and sliced potatoes. The problem was, we weren't paying enough attention and the pot of grease started smoking a lot. Things went from bad to worse when we went to move it to the sink. The pot caught fire, and putting water on it only made the flames shoot up! When the kitchen curtains caught, I frantically pulled them down, put them in the second sink, and turned on the water. That fire went out, and Chris told me to grab the flaming pot and bring it outside. He ran to the door and, thinking he was going to hold it open for me, I threw the pot. But Chris hadn't held the door, he was running *through* it. By that time, it was too late and the flaming pot of grease hit him in the back.

It was horrible. I still remember him yelling in agony, "Let me die in peace!" while I helped him get his shirt off, and quite a bit of his skin along with it.

Again I called my aunt to come to the rescue. One of her older boys told me to get Chris in a tub of cool water and they were on their way. They brought Chris to the hospital and thankfully he was okay. I carried the guilt about hurting him for a long time. In fact, it wasn't until years later that I wondered why he didn't carry the flaming pot himself. He was older than I was. He should have told me to hold the door; he should have protected me by carrying the pot with a blazing fire in it. I also realized how lucky we were that we didn't burn the house down with the other kids sleeping. I know I would have died trying to save them, and I can only wonder if Chris would have helped me.

That was also the year I got my first job. It was at an Italian restaurant. I walked over every Saturday morning and peeled garlic for several hours, for which I was paid a princely five dollars a week. Even better, I got a reprieve from watching the other kids. I did buy stuff for the family with my earnings, things like ice-cream and a pack of ice-cream cones or popcorn and Kool-Aid so we'd have snacks in the evenings. Things that we used to have before we moved. In this hard new world, they brought us comfort and familiarity.

I was lonely in that house; it was on a busy commercial street so there were no kids around. Fortunately, we didn't stay there too long. We'd soon move to a new house in a new town, but with its own set of problems.

Haverstraw

First, I lost my job. For a few weeks after we moved Dad had driven me to the restaurant, but it was twenty minutes away – too inconvenient to drive back and forth twice or wait for me to be done with my shift. I understood, but I was not happy about losing my job and my income.

Second, being home more meant I had to deal more with Chris, who had continued to run amok. He had started smoking pot and drinking and often disrupted my efforts to get the kids to do homework and take baths.

Things were pretty rough for us, and they were about to get rougher. For me, they went sideways after we moved for the fourth time that year. I caught Chris smoking pot and told him I was going to tell Dad. He replied by threatening to tell Dad that I was a slut and "Dad wouldn't believe a slut."

No way Dad will buy that, I thought. I had never even kissed a boy yet, had never been on a date. On the other hand, if he did believe Chris it would really hurt him. My dad loved me and wanted me to be a "nice girl."

I took my time deciding what to do about the situation. It seemed my parents had no control over Chris' behavior, and their attention was so focused on paying the bills I didn't think they would try hard enough to change anything. In the end, though I knew his behavior was wrong, I decided not to bother telling Mom and Dad about his drug use and just be grateful the younger boys were not with him.

Imagine my surprise when my father came to me and said, "Sweetie, I need to talk to you." He then proceeded to tell me, that according to Chris, everyone at school was talking about me being a tramp.

"How could you do this?" Dad said, "My daughter is a pig. I raised you better than that!"

I couldn't believe that despite my silence Chris had gone through with his threat.

"He's lying, Dad! I have never done anything with any boys. I am planning on being a nun! Don't believe him!"

My plea fell on deaf ears.

"Why would he say something like that, if it weren't true?" Dad asked. "Chris is ashamed and embarrassed because everyone is talking about his sister. Nobody will bring a pig home to their mother."

There was more to it, but the bottom line was that my dad had lost respect for me and he was the light of my life. How the heck had this happened? How could I fix it? What gross thing could he possibly think I had done?

God, please help him to believe me and love me again.

I really was an innocent little girl and didn't know there was much more than kissing. To this day, it makes me sick to think what my dad must have thought I did. It is also very sad that my brother had put that hurt on my parents and on me. On the other hand, I have never understood how Dad could believe Chris over me. He was so bad, and I was responsible, and good. That hurt me for a long time. I still didn't tell my parents about the pot ... why bother? My dad didn't even believe me about my own reputation, so why would he believe anything else I had to say?

There were train tracks that ran right behind the house we were living in. One day, Chris hopped a train and threw a bunch of cases of Winston cigarettes, each filled with several cartons, right by our yard. This resulted in two things: my parents got into the cigarette business for a while, earning much-needed extra money, and my brothers all started smoking. I wanted to stop them – they were so young – but it was no use. At least I kept the girls away from the woods so they couldn't start, thank you, God, but for the life of me I couldn't keep Chris away from the boys. The truth was, they liked to be with him, they liked to do bad things. In one year, I had watched our family, and happy little life, fall apart.

I missed Mr. Roy and my school and my church and my neighbors back in Oregon. I had a few new friends but not many, mostly because the kids on our block had money to spend and I had nothing. I couldn't go get lunch at the pizza place or hang out after school or go to the movies or skating. How I wished I had a job again! I wished I knew kids to sell the cigarettes to like Chris and my parents did. I bet I would have, even though I knew that stealing and selling cigarettes was wrong.

That summer we moved yet again, this time to Alice Street in Garnerville, not far from Haverstraw, also in Rockland County. I didn't mind leaving the old place as I had never really gotten settled there, and at least this time I would be starting a new school at the beginning of the year. I just hoped this move was the last one – two states and four different schools in nine months was more than enough.

Socially, the move made things much better for me. I made friends, lots of them, right away. I liked my new seventh-grade classmates and there were lots of kids on our street. But it was on Alice Street that I also saw my little brother Mickey, then about ten years old, drunk. I will never forget seeing him staggering down the block.

"Who did this to you?!" I yelled at him, but he was so wasted he couldn't even answer. I got him home and into bed so he wouldn't get in trouble, then I walked up to the schoolyard, which was where he had come from. No one was around, and I just stood there, fuming that someone had done this to my baby brother.

Thanks to Chris, things were not going well for any of the boys. He had taught them to steal and they would leave together, no matter how much I begged the younger ones to stay with me. They wanted Chris's approval, even though he beat all of us up all the time and was mean to them whenever he felt like it. They loved him and thought he was cool. Truth be told, I loved Chris too, but didn't think he was cool at all. I just wanted him to either be good or go away and leave the rest of us alone.

One day Chris showed up while we were watching our twelve-inch black and white tv.

"Come on, you guys," he said, "let's go steal some candy and stuff."

The boys eagerly went to the door to join him.

"No, Chris," I shouted, "Leave them here! Mickey, Timmy, you guys stay here with me. You don't need to go get in trouble with him. I have twenty cents. We can go to the corner store and get something later."

"Tell her to shut up," Chris said, then turned to me and snapped, "Shut up, pig."

It was one of his favorite things to call me. He knew how much it hurt.

We played this verbal tug-of-war with the boys for a few minutes, and I was losing.

"Come on, you don't have to listen to her. Let's go."

Timmy was already out of my reach so I grabbed Mickey's shoulders and tried to turn him back toward the house. That's when it literally became a tug-of-war, with Chris pulling Mickey's upper body while I held his legs. Chris was stronger than me, and I cried with frustration as I was dragged down the steps. Still, I wouldn't give up.

"Leave him here, he's NOT going."

"Yes, he is," Chris said, with a kick and a stomp on my back, so hard it completely knocked the wind out of me and I had to let go.

Mick turned around and said, "I'm sorry, Peg," and I knew he meant it. I loved those boys so much and I wanted them to have a good life, not the one Chris was leading them into. I had lost another battle and could only hope and pray I didn't lose the war.

The World on My Shoulders

Next door there lived an Italian family, the Cassellas, that turned out to be a great blessing for me. The parents were older than mine and they had two married children – a son, Peter, and a daughter, Paula, who was about ten years older than me. A dog named Belle completed the perfect picture. Mr. and Mrs. Casella lived half the year in Florida and half in New York, which

I thought was the coolest thing I'd ever heard of and hoped to do one day.

One year, just when they were about to go to Florida, Paula and her husband and two daughters moved in. I loved Paula; she was a breath of fresh air. I could talk to her about all kinds of stuff, and she treated me like a teenager, not some little kid. Smart and kind, Paula gave me hope that life wouldn't always be like this. She ordered clothes for me from the Sears catalog and tweezed my bushy eyebrows. She bought me makeup and taught me how to put it on. Thank you, God, for putting her in my life and for letting me feel special. I needed it!

Little did I know a disaster, and our greatest challenge, was right around the corner.

It seemed like a good thing when Mom got a job at a factory close enough to walk to from our house. I don't think she was there long when her hand was smashed by a machine. And I mean *smashed*, as in completely useless and disfigured for life, despite many surgeries. The doctors made it look like a hand using immovable pins and skin from her thighs, but it was not really a hand anymore.

The day it happened we were home waiting and wondering why she wasn't home yet. It was Mrs. Casella who broke the news: Mom had had an accident and was in the hospital; she wouldn't be home for a long time. Mrs. Casella fed us dinner that night. We were all so sad.

I remember after getting all the kids to bed that night, I went to sit out front on the stoop. Mrs. Casella walked over and told me I was going to have to help more now. That I would have to take care of things. I would have a lot more responsibility. Hearing that, I just about cried my guts out. I was a kid and already missing my mom, and now I was going to have to take care of everything? What hospital was she in, and when would my dad get home? What the heck was I supposed to do with all this work and all these kids? They didn't even listen to me.

"Stop crying," Mrs. Casella said, "You can and will take care of this house and the kids; you are well able. Besides, you are not crying for your mother right now. You are crying for yourself."

Maybe I was, but I was scared.

Mom was gone for months and as Mrs. Casella had predicted I completely took responsibility for the household. It was a lot, but I enjoyed cooking and was happy to learn all I could about seasoning and spices. All we had ever used was salt. We did have a can of black pepper in the back of the cupboard, but I wasn't allowed to use it. Now that I was "in charge" I could do what I wanted, so I started using pepper and other spices I got from the neighbor or purchased with my own money. I earned five dollars a week for cleaning, cooking, and making sure the kids got home from school. I also had a little money from babysitting for Paula on occasion. Spending it on food was worth it to me – I got to try out new recipes and we all sat down and ate together as a family every night. Well, except for Chris who was usually out doing God-knows-what. And that was just fine by me.

Sometimes I went for weeks without a penny to my name. We had few clothes and holes in our shoes – we'd have to put cardboard in the bottoms and plastic bags over our feet to keep the rain and snow out. Once, I was so tired of having nothing that I stole sixteen dollars from my teacher's desk. I will never forget it as long as I live. I justified my actions because I didn't take it from a person. I wanted to bring it back, but didn't. It felt terrible.

Mom was in and out of the hospital, often gone for several months at a time, and we didn't see her much. At one point she was staying at the convent with her sister, Sister Agnes, and we were told she just needed time to adjust to losing a hand. She got down to ninety pounds. After a while she went from being in and out of the hospital to being in and out of rehab. At least that was in walking distance so we could go visit her.

Those were the days when women raised their daughters to have their own families, and Mom must have done a good job with me because I was managing to hold it all together. I was also becoming a woman and wanted my privacy. I had none – not my own room or even a bed to myself. I always shared with Nancy, who was a few years younger than me, and though we got along great I just wanted some time alone once in a while.

When I got my period I was on my own. Dad had no sense of what I needed and I didn't know how to ask (I also knew he didn't have the money for such things), so I just went to the store and bought pads. I also went behind his back and bought some Nair hair remover. I wasn't allowed to shave but they'd never said I couldn't use Nair. It worked! All the long black hair on my legs was gone. I felt terrific. Then Chris went through my room and found it in my hiding space, along with Loves Baby soft cologne, a tweezer, and my stash of cooking spices. He then showed everything to Dad, but, unlike when he told the lie about my "promiscuity," he didn't get the reaction he had hoped for. Dad did think I was too young for hair remover, however. How could he not realize I was one of the hairiest girls he'd ever seen?

"Dad, please," I said, "I bought it with my own money. All the other girls at my school get to shave!"

"Peggy, you're wasting your money on things like this. You don't need it."

"I *do* need it! I am so hairy and why isn't Chris in trouble for searching through my room?"

"Stay out of her room, Chris."

After some negotiation, I was told I had to keep the spices in the kitchen; I could keep the perfume and, after much pleading, I was allowed to keep the Nair!

Though Dad had seen my side that time, I was reaching a breaking point. No one could control Chris, and Nancy let the other kids in our room all the time. I needed my own space.

A Startling Discovery Here

I went up into the attic to see if I could make it into a bedroom for myself. Maybe, I thought, if I came up with a good plan my dad would let me have the space. There was a set of stairs that unfolded when you pulled a door down from the upstairs hallway. Using an extension cord and a hanger to pull down the stairs, I climbed up and started going through everything, dropping the stuff I could get rid of down the steps and putting the rest to the back corner. I made my way back through the Christmas boxes and stacked them neatly. Then, much to my surprise, I found a bunch of purses I had never seen before. I figured the previous owners of the house must have left them.

After getting everything straightened out, dusted off, and vacuumed, I hung up a sheet to separate the storage from my new space and climbed backward down those old rickety stairs to clean up the giant mess below. I had a box and some paper bags to put the junk in and started putting one purse inside of the other. That is when I realized there were things in them – important things, including wallets with IDs and other items, all from different women. These weren't discarded purses left by the previous tenants, so how did they get here?

Suddenly I was overcome with dread. *Not you, Chris,* I thought, my heart sinking. *How could you do this?* There had been a lot of talk around town about little old ladies getting knocked down by a purse snatcher. Could it really be my brother? How could he do this? There were seven or eight purses, seven or eight old ladies he'd stolen from. Seven or eight ladies he may have hurt.

A whirlwind of thoughts took over my mind. *What am I supposed to do now? Call the police? I know my parents would want me to talk to Dad first, but he has so many problems right now with Mom not home. What should I do? Should I just take care of this and tell Peter Casella? He's a policeman. Chris will probably go to jail, but my parents will be so sad and embarrassed. No, I can't tell Peter yet. Dad will be home after he visits Mom; he will know what to do.*

I hid the purses under my bed – the little kids didn't need to know about this – and later told my dad. Needless to say, he was furious... but that was it. I never saw the bags again. Chris didn't go to jail. We never talked about it again. It's hard to fathom looking back, but I had to keep sharing the bedroom, and bed, with Nancy and Chris got the room in the attic. He was the oldest. The only other recollection I have of that big room in the attic is of Chris up there, enjoying the space with his friend Butch. I smelled pot and went up there to tell them to get out and stop bringing drugs around the house. He held me down while Butch blew the smoke in my face. For the first time in my life, I was stoned.

My seventh-grade year rolled into the next and things at home were the same. Chris was still beating me up anytime he felt like it and causing mayhem whenever he was around. No money, unavailable parents, food to purchase and cook, laundry to do, and lots of kids to take care of. Mom wasn't there much – she was still in and out of the hospital or rehab – and I'm not too sure she even wanted to be. It was like she'd lost her place at the house. She was physically and emotionally distraught, no doubt because she was trying desperately to deal with losing the use of her right – and dominant – hand. She had a big cast and a sling on her right arm and had one surgery after another. I'm sure she needed counseling, a friend, and some help around the house, and she had none of the above. Well, she had my help, but I was sick of it. They weren't *my* kids. I'm sure we tried our best to be good and quiet and help out, but with seven kids Mom couldn't catch a break. She just needed much more than any of us had to give. No wonder she had to find rest and reprieve at a convent.

As for me, it took all I had to navigate teen life with acne and a poor self-esteem. I was spent, trying to survive day by day. I still had some vague aspirations of joining the convent to do God's work, but by that point it was fading, though I would have seized any opportunity to live anywhere but that crazy house. The truth was, I couldn't leave. The little kids only had me and what would happen to them if I left? Anyway, I wouldn't have been able to go even if Mom was okay, because I was too young. According to my dad, you now had to be eighteen to join the convent, not like in the olden days when Sister Agnes went; she was only fifteen. Still, I went to church and religion classes and did my best to keep all the younger kids going too.

Chris never went to church anymore, and when he was around he made sure the boys skipped it too. I don't know why he wanted them to be bad except misery loves company. I will never know the answer to what Chris thought or why he behaved the way he did. I do know he mapped the course for all of us and overwhelmed our parents and zapped all their energy. Chris ruled everything, and if things were going well, it was because he wasn't home. If there were fistfights or someone getting beaten, high or drunk, Chris was most likely around.

I think we all had a feeling of being "less than." When someone is allowed to steal from you, beat you up, calls you names, and tell you that you are stupid, fat and ugly, it hurts. Even worse, you begin to feel stupid, fat, and ugly – at least I did. I knew better, but nobody stopped the abuse. Nobody told any family secrets. I will never understand why my parents let it happen. They must have realized that they sacrificed the emotional health and well-being of the six because they didn't know what to do with the number one son. Chris was put into a home for boys for a while, and we used to visit him there. I can't tell you what he did to get there – he was such a deviant it could have been anything. Many secrets were kept in our family.

One time I was sitting on the front stoop and Chris came running around the corner and into the house with a man's pants – belt, wallet, and underwear attached. He told me he was hitchhiking and the guy had tried to do something to him, but I never knew when Chris was telling me the truth. I do know that when he was away we had a semblance of peace. Yes, there was a lot of dysfunctions in the home, with Mom gone most of the time and the two younger boys starting to kick up – but at least Chris wasn't beating the crap out of me and Mickey.

Mick loved attention and caused trouble sometimes with his smart mouth. He never knew when to shut up. Then he told us that one teacher was tying him up and putting him in the closet, day after day. Was it true? I went up to his classroom and, sure enough, I found him in there, tied, gagged, and screaming and fighting against his restraints. The teacher dragged me to the office, where I got a referral for skipping school! When my parents heard of this, I got a stern, "This is no way to deal with things. Don't let it happen again!" Why they didn't fight for us? I will never know. On the bright side, Mick was never tied up again, thank you, Lord.

True Love

Life was much the same when I got to high school, with one big exception: I had met my first true love. His name was Jody Pilcher. It happened at the end of eighth grade. I was with a friend named Jeanne, and she wanted to go to visit a friend in Samsondale, a neighborhood with pretty rows of three and four bedroom townhouses about a mile away from where I lived. Until then my only experience with Samsondale had been cutting through it to go to the nearest grocery store. It was a small development but full of life because of all the kids that lived there, as well as a busy shopping center with a few restaurants and a movie theater. The neighborhood backed up to a park with swings, equipment, and basketball hoops. A stream ran along the park and behind the stream were the woods.

That day, Jeanne and I went to meet her friend Margarette in the park, the entrance of which was about three or four doors from her house. As we strolled up the walkway between two sets of row houses that led to the park, there he was: a boy I had never seen before, working on a car. The hood of the car was up and he was bent over the engine with a tool in his hand. As he looked up, our eyes met, or more accurately, they *locked*. We both smiled. He stood up from his bent position and watched me as I walked into the park. I don't know what hit me, but though we didn't say a word, the chemistry between us was overpowering.

Who is that guy? Did he feel the same thing I did? What happened in that moment that I can't explain? I can remember it exactly, just like it was yesterday, and I will tell you the truth: I never dreamed of being a nun again.

My new friend felt it too.

"Wow" Margarette said, "he likes you!"

"Oh my gosh!" I said, "Who is he?"

Jeanne, always the voice of reason, replied, "Peggy. It doesn't matter who he is! Your dad doesn't even want you talking to Puerto Ricans and that guy is black. Forget it. Don't go near him."

But I wasn't listening; it was too late.

You know, I don't even remember what happened next or how we made contact again, but that was it. He was my boyfriend and we were in love. Of course, Jeanne was right. My parents weren't happy about my first boyfriend at all, and their little girl, who had never caused problems for anyone, was about to start. I had always been the good one, always doing what I was supposed to be doing. But suddenly I had something in my life I had never experienced or expected: the romantic love of a boy who I loved deeply in return. It was amazing, and if I had my way, Jody and I would have been together day and night.

Despite what Jeanne said, I'm not sure why my parents were so upset. I'd like to believe that it wasn't just his color, or that they had lost their twenty-four-hour cook and babysitter. I would rather think they were worried because I was so young and impressionable, and so crazy for this guy. Whatever the case, they were seeing a new me. Though I'd always had friends, I always came home early; I was always there to help. Now I was less involved with the family, though I still found plenty of time to help around the house. I just wasn't there the minute I got home from school and then all night. I still had time to hang out with my friends on the block or go to a friend's house after school. Then I would come home, have dinner with the family, and do whatever needed to be done.

Jody came to the house to try to get to know them, but it didn't work, and the more I spent time with him the more my parents resisted. We honestly didn't do anything except go to the mall or the park and hang out a little bit; or, if he had money, we'd get a hamburger. But the most fun we had was driving around in his car, listening to music and singing along. We had so much fun together, just being together and talking. It was great.

We did get into a bit of mischief once in a while. One night we were driving around and ended up at the schoolyard near my house. It was raining, and the schoolyard was soaked. Jody decided to do cookies out in that grass. I had never done anything like that; I'd never had a friend who had a car. It was fun, but I didn't like the destruction it caused.

Jody was two grades older and much worldlier than I was. I was a sweet girl who stayed home every day, and though I wouldn't call myself super-innocent, I was rather naïve. Yes, I knew there was a lot of bad stuff going on out there, and that Jody was kind of a bad boy, but I certainly didn't see it that way. True, he didn't mind getting in a fight here and there. But all in all he was a great guy – smart and strong, loving, extra charming and oh-so-cool, especially from the perspective of my fifteen-year-old eyes and heart. I couldn't have been happier. On the other hand, my parents were putting more and more restrictions on me. I was still getting good grades and I was still helping at home. I was still an awesome big sister to my siblings. Yet the fights at home became more and more frequent.

"Why can't I go? I am fifteen and shouldn't have to be home at eight-thirty. It's not even dark out yet."

"You're not going out, Peggy."

"You can't keep me from him, I am not a prisoner!"

"You have school, Peggy. You have responsibilities here; you just can't go tootling off any time you feel like it."

Being a resourceful young woman, I found a different way out. My upstairs bedroom was across from the bathroom. I would climb out the bathroom window onto the porch roof, then jump several feet to the branch of a nearby tree. From there, it was a short drop to the ground.

This was back before the days of cell phones and texting, so all Jody and I could do was plan to meet at a certain place and time. Since Jody worked, it was generally ten p.m. at the church parking lot across the street and down the block from my house. I would come back in by one or two, get as much sleep as I could before school the next morning, and no one was the wiser. This lasted for about three or four months and was working marvelously. Yes, I felt awful going against my parents, but I certainly wasn't going to give Jody up.

One night, I went out onto the porch roof from the bathroom and jumped out onto the branch, as I had so many times before. But this time, as I leaped in the air and grabbed the branch, it snapped! I fell flat on my back – a pretty hard fall from the porch roof – and the branch landed on top of me. The wind was knocked from my lungs and I just lay there for a moment, trying to catch my breath. Thankfully, though it hurt, I knew I was okay and slowly got to my feet. Then, since I couldn't leave the branch in the front yard, I picked it up and dragged it over to the parking lot where Jody was waiting. It was really dark but he could see me pulling something and he got out of the car.

"What happened, what are you doing with that?"

When I told him what happened he burst out laughing, so hard he almost cried. Then he helped me drag the branch over the parking lot and into the woods where nobody would notice it. But the problem was not the broken branch, the problem was that my only way out of the house after curfew was gone. I needed to get a new escape plan figured out right away!

Things did not work out very well after that. Turns out there was no other way of sneaking out of the house. My parents refused to budge on the curfew, and if I wasn't home on time they would drive down to Samsondale and look for me. Or they would call around to all my friends and somebody always knew where I was. This made things very hard and very uncomfortable, and soon Jody and I were skipping school so we could see each other and go to his house, which was empty because his parents both worked. I felt awful skipping school because I was a great student and actually liked it, but I loved him more.

For a while this worked out really well. I was easily able to catch up on any work I missed, and I became an expert in copying my mom's signature. But of course things like this always catch up with you. I never considered the school calling or sending a letter home, but that's what they did. My parents learned that their daughter, who'd always had perfect attendance, was suddenly missing two and three days of school per week. Naturally, they blamed Jody because I'd never gotten into trouble before. The problem, I didn't care; I only wanted to see Jody.

It wasn't as bad for Jody. His parents weren't happy about what was going on, but there was less they could do because he was turning eighteen soon. He was concerned about me getting into trouble, but since he wanted to see me he went along with it. So I continued skipping, and soon found myself in hot water for truancy – especially after the principal, Mr. Sepulveda, figured out that I had been signing my mom's name.

"Peggy," he said, "you are such a smart girl and your grades have been good. Why are you doing this? You know you're ruining your high school education."

I don't know what I told him, but it wasn't the truth. I knew it was wrong, I knew it was stupid. I didn't know how to explain that he was more important and I just didn't want to give up what I had. I finally felt like I was loved. There was nothing more important to me in the whole wide world.

"I've given you chance after chance of making up your grades so that you can pass everything but you haven't accepted my help. You don't have a reason to be here right now because you're not passing most of the classes. You can sign yourself out at sixteen. What do you want to do? I will not let you come and go as you please. You commit to the curriculum or stay home."

"I guess I'll just quit then."

I know – stupid, stupid, stupid.

My parents were furious and told me to get a job, so I did, in the cafeteria of the Sears at the Nanuet Mall.

One day, after I had been there for about a week, I went to the little back office to let John, the supervisor, know I was leaving. He got out of his chair, walked over to me, cupped my breasts, and gently twisted my nipples.

"You are a very beautiful girl. Do you know that?"

I have no idea what I said, or if I even said anything. I just ran out of there as fast as I could. I felt disgusting, humiliated; I just couldn't believe what he had done. I guess that's where my naivety comes in; I honestly never knew that somebody could be such a pig. I had never heard of this happening to anyone before. Why did he do it to me? What had I done to prompt that?

Jody picked me up from work and I did not tell him what happened. I felt like it was somehow my fault and I really didn't know what to do or say about it – especially since my aunt had helped me get the job and I didn't want it to reflect badly on her. I couldn't go back there. What would stop that from happening again?

I continued to agonize about it for the next few days. Should I tell my parents? What was I supposed to do? Finally, knowing I needed to talk to someone, I did end up telling Jody. He was probably the wrong person. I should not have gone to him for help, but that's what I did.

Not surprisingly, he was irate, and I called and quit without notice. I should have reported the guy, but I wasn't raised to stick up for myself, and I also didn't want to admit to anyone else what had happened to me. I was really mortified. Totally ashamed.

When payday came, I called to make sure my check was ready, then went to pick it up when I knew he wasn't alone. I didn't want to face him again. When I returned to the car, Jody said, I'll be right back. I found out later that he went in and asked for the supervisor.

"Are you John?" Jody asked when the man came to the counter.

"Yes, I am. How can I help you?"

Without another word, Jody punched him square in the face, breaking his glasses, then left the restaurant. He came back out to the car and drove away, his adrenaline pumping. I was nervous; I just wanted to get my paycheck, not cause any trouble.

And I had bigger problems: I wasn't in school, had no job and no plan. How had I let this happen? How would I get myself back together? I just hated being a burden on my parents like Chris was, but they had refused to listen to my feelings and let me have a boyfriend like other girls. I couldn't believe I was barely sixteen and my life had gotten so bad.

Chapter Three

ANOTHER UNEXPECTED MOVE

Things changed drastically for me in June 1978. After years of struggling my parents couldn't take it in New York anymore and decided we were moving back to Oregon. My dad got a job, and I and two of my brothers, Timmy and Mickey, drove out west with him. Mom and the other girls stayed behind for a few months until we got settled. I was so sad to leave the life I knew, but mostly because I had to leave Jody. I begged to stay in New York with Mom and the girls, but that of course was a hard no. I had made my life a shambles, with not much to fight for except his love.

We made tearful plans. We weren't breaking up; we were getting married! He was going to come to Oregon and get me when I turned eighteen. *Oh God,* I prayed, *please let this be true. I love him so much. Hopefully things will work out better when they see how much he loves me.*

I am not sure where Chris was at this time. Dad and my two younger brothers moved into a big house with my aunt and three of her kids. I had my cousin Jimmy, who was my age. We were very different but he was kind and he loved me – a friend when I needed one desperately. He would let me play my Meatloaf album and sing to him while I jumped on his bed and danced around his room. In fact, to this day Jim still loves and supports me in all my endeavors.

I just had one friend left from childhood, Anna. We had written a few times and she even came out one summer to visit us in New York. She still lived in the same house and had the same neighbors: the Carnleys, who had four kids I also used to know, Kevin and his three sisters.

Anna wasn't the same girl she'd been when I left Oregon. She was wild: sex, drinking, smoking, drugs. I had barely done much of anything while I was in New York, and she let me know that my goody two shoes, I'm-not-having-sex-till-I'm-married ways wouldn't fly out in the Wild West.

After months of separation, Mom and the girls finally came out. Dad was established at a good job and found a house to buy in Portland. It was nice to get a fresh start, and be in our own house again. It was close to the few friends I made, and I got a job at a burger place and started making money right away. I wasn't returning to school though. I had told my parents that if they made me leave New York I wasn't going to start over in my junior year with no friends. I have no idea why I was the one calling the shots – I was only sixteen! – but they agreed that if I got a job and paid rent I could quit school. I think life was just getting to be too much for my parents. I didn't feel great about my decision, but I had made it and, in my mind, there was no going back. I liked my job, I paid them rent, and life went on.

We hadn't moved to the best neighborhood and I didn't meet the best people working a minimum wage job. I did, however, meet a cute guy named Mark. He had a girlfriend named Bobbie, which was okay because I knew Jody would come to get me in a few years. If anyone asked, I had a boyfriend. I got lots of attention because of my New York accent, which I enjoyed, but I was definitely intent on waiting for my man. Then, a few months later, I received a letter from my good friend Marc from Samsondale that broke my heart and changed everything.

Jody is not keeping his promise to you. He has already had a few girlfriends. Don't waste your life waiting for him. He doesn't deserve you.

Marc was gentle and kind and broke the bad news in a much nicer way, but that was the gist of it, and it was like a stab to the heart. As much as I didn't want to believe it and had no evidence, I knew it was true. Jody was handsome and a flirt, and girls liked him. Plus, Marc and Jody were good friends and Marc would never lie about him, or want to hurt me like that for no reason. I decided to go out with Mark, the boy from work. But first, I wrote Jody a letter.

Dear Jody,

I love you very much and I can't wait to see you again. I realize we are very young and two years is a long time to wait. I have decided to go out with a boy named Mark Smith that I met at work. I promise I will not fall in love with him. If you have, or want to go out with someone else, please don't fall in love with her either. I will be waiting for you and I still want you to come for me when I turn eighteen so we can get married.

Love Always,

Peggy

For our first date, Mark took me to see Black Sabbath and Van Halen. We had a good time, and after that he just kind of became my boyfriend. I didn't have that crazy-in-love feeling like I did with Jody. I actually figured I'd never have that magic again. But we hung out and partied a lot with the other kids we worked with, until I got a new job. I kept working, kept paying my parents rent.

Unfortunately, Chris then came back into the picture. I didn't know where he had been – Mom said it was the army, but it could have been jail – I didn't know, I didn't care. Life hadn't been good for any of us but at least Chris wasn't there, causing chaos and beating us up and stealing from me. Now he had returned, and he picked up right where he left off.

I decided I was going to get out of there as soon as I could. I was saving up money and I kept it hidden under my mattress. One night I was fast asleep when Chris came into my room and flipped the mattress over with me on it. I found myself laying on the floor with the mattress on top of me, while Chris grabbed the envelope full of money – one hundred and eighty dollars – and ran away with it. I had no way to stop him. I was stunned and crushed, and so angry with myself for telling the other kids about my money. I made barely two dollars an hour and paid rent out of that, saving most of what I had left. And now it was gone forever.

One day Chris was sitting in the front room and I was in the entry with my friend, Joan, who was fixing my hair.

"It doesn't matter what you do," he said, "you will always be ugly."

"Leave me alone, Chris."

"Why, does the truth hurt?"

"Shut up, Chris, and leave me alone. Why don't you get out of here?"

"Don't tell me to shut up, you ugly pig."

"Shut up!" I shouted. I was trying to have some dignity in front of my friend. I really should have kept my mouth shut.

Chris bolted across the room and smashed a heavy carnival glass ashtray over my head. When I fell to the ground, bleeding, he picked up the fallen cigarette butts and stuffed them in my mouth. It was a hell of a beating, even from him.

Joan ran to get a towel and find my mom while Chris stepped back.

My mom came out and said, "Peggy, why can't you get along with him? There's always trouble when you're around!"

"Yeah," Chris said, "you're a troublemaker."

Hurt, stunned and crying, I left the house pressing a bath towel to the gash on my head. Even after everything that had happened over the years, I couldn't believe it. Why was he so mean to me? How could she take his side? Did Joan tell her what he had done to me? I walked to the hospital a few miles away with that bloody towel on my head. I told them what happened and that my parents had insurance. I'm not sure if they verified it or anything, but they took care of me and put me in a room. There was a really nice lady asking me questions. When I got the wound somewhat cleaned up and a few stitches in my head, she came in with the police to ask me the same questions again. Oh no! What had I done? I don't want to cause any more trouble for my family. I don't want the kids to get taken away.

"Oh no," I assured them, "you must have misunderstood." Then I continued rambling, saying anything to stop them from looking deeper into what was going on in my house.

"It wasn't my brother. I think it was someone my brother knows."

"No, I don't know his name."

"I'm okay, I was being a smart mouth."

"I started it; I was asking for it."

"No sir, I don't need a ride home I am going to spend the night with my friend here."

Bob, Joan's dad, came and picked us up and took me to their house. I was afraid to go home. There was no controlling Chris; he did anything he wanted, there was no way to punish him and Mom wasn't about to kick him out. I feared the next fight could be the death of me – literally.

Joan's parents were such a blessing. They had an extra room and let me move in; they didn't even charge me rent. I could have gone to my aunt's house but it was an hour away from my job. I was working at McDonald's and didn't have a car or any hope of driving any time soon, so Joan's dad, God bless him, drove me to work every morning about five-forty a.m. on the way to his own job. It was perfect timing for the breakfast shift, six a.m. to two p.m., which I worked Monday through Friday. I loved it. I was really good at it. I made friends with the regulars, young and old.

Joan's mom Beth was a lovely woman but an alcoholic and drunk most nights. The home was very dysfunctional, but at least it wasn't physically abusive. With all this going on nobody really paid attention to what else was happening to the girls in the house. There were three of us, Joan, her sister Lucy, and me. Joan had a room in the basement and her boyfriend Jim lived there with her, though Beth and Bob really didn't know it. Jim had been kicked out of his parents' house and just moved in. Neither Jim nor Joan worked, so they just stayed in her room whenever Bob was home or Beth was having her coffee. After noon each day Beth would go back to her room and start drinking, so they came upstairs for food. It was really a sad existence for everyone, but I told myself it was still better than being home.

I spent a lot of time with Lucy, especially in evenings – we would sit on the floor doing sit-ups, stretches and other exercises while we watched tv and talked. Bob would either be working on the printing press downstairs or in the bedroom with Beth; Joan was usually out or downstairs with Jim. I couldn't do anything during the week because Bob and I left for work before dawn and I was determined to never make him wait for me.

Then there was Mike, the older brother, who didn't live there but came over a lot. He was about twenty-four years old, seven or eight years older than me, and a fun guy. He was kind and a hard- worker; he loved his family. He worked with his hands, a roofer or framer, I believe. Oh, and he was so handsome, strong and tan.

Mike would often come over after work to visit the family. Depending on Beth's condition he'd either go into her room or she'd come out and sit at the dining room table with him. You could see how much she adored him. He was momma's golden boy, the light of her life, and it was nice when she was able to stay sober enough for his visits. I remember thinking how great it would be to have a big brother like that, and how lucky they were that he cared about all of them so much. He always brought laughter into the house, and I really enjoyed becoming friends with him. It never occurred to me that this "nice guy" would want something more.

One night I was asleep in my room when Mike came in and got in bed with me. I could smell the alcohol on his breath.

"Mike, no, please get out," I said, startled. "Why are you in here? What are you doing?"

"I want to be with you," he replied, kissing me and holding me tight.

"Well, go to sleep. I'm not doing anything with you. I have a boyfriend. I don't cheat on people."

"C'mon Peggy, I love you. Don't you love me too? I know you do, I can tell."

"No, I don't, and you have a girlfriend!"

"I'm going to breakup with her. I want to be with you."

"No, I don't want to. Mike, please get off me. Get out of my room. You're hurting me. I'm not doing this with you."

"I'm not going to hurt you, just stop fighting me. I love you and, yes, yes you are..."

He forced himself on me and yes, I could have screamed and fought, but I didn't. A million thoughts were racing through my head. How could I cause all this trouble in this house and expect to stay here? The answer was, I couldn't. Beth would never believe her golden boy would do anything wrong. She thought he hung the moon. If I told anyone what happened, and he lied and said I was willing Beth would kick me out. Then what? I had a room, food, and a ride to work. His parents were right across the hall, and I was being raped and letting it happen. How had I gotten myself into this mess of a life? I had been saving all my money to get an apartment, but it wasn't happening fast enough; I need to move out ASAP.

For the next few months, Mike came in my room at least once or twice a week. I felt like a prostitute, selling my body for a place to live. I hated it, and I hated myself. I could have gone back home, but I didn't. I could have found someone who may have helped me, but who? I considered telling Jim, but he would have told his stepfather and then all hell would break loose. And what would Joan say, after her parents had taken me in, in my hour of need? Was I to drop a bomb in the middle of the already unstable family? How unfair would that be? I didn't want to put Bob in that position, even though I didn't know what a good marriage looked like I knew he and Beth's couldn't withstand this kind of turmoil. Or, what if I told Bob and he didn't believe me? He was my lifeline, driving me to work and not even expecting me to pay rent. It was in many ways far better than my own house, where I had to share a room and we didn't always have food.

I also knew I could call the police, but then what? I didn't want Mike to go to jail. Except for the forceful sex I honestly liked the guy... maybe I even loved him, or so I thought. I didn't want him to be punished... I just wanted him to stop. I knew it wasn't right – not for me, not for his girlfriend, not for my boyfriend Mark or my true love, Jody.

My biggest fear was that God would be ashamed of me. I knew I wasn't supposed to have sex out of wedlock, yet there I was, having sex with a guy who was not even a boyfriend.

I was seventeen when I finally got my own apartment. I had to lie about the year I was born, but it was within walking distance of McDonald's and just five blocks from my parents so my little brothers and sisters could visit. After a while I got a better, full-time job as a cashier in a cafeteria at a bank in downtown Portland. I think I made four-fifty an hour – almost two dollars more than I had made at McDonald's – plus benefits and free lunch every day.

I helped Willie, the supervisor, with food prep along with taking care of the coffee, but my main job was breakfast and lunch cashiering. After lunch, I counted the money, helped clean up and went downstairs to make the bank deposit. I missed McDonalds, but it was worth it because I had my eye on a bank teller position. For that, I would need a high school diploma which, thanks to my stubbornness the year before, I didn't have. It was too late now; my life was going well and I needed the money to pay my rent. No way I could quit work to go back to school. That would mean moving back home. It was not an option.

At the time I was still dating Mark, and he would come over after work and spend the night. He wanted to move in officially, and though I loved having him there I didn't want to be a girl who lives with a man without being married. I know it seems ridiculous after the situation I had just gotten out of, but this was different. It would have been my choice, rather than coercion, and certainly would make God even more unhappy. My dad, I knew, would want to kill me.

I used to think, *Maybe one day we will get married. He can chip in on the bills and I can work less and go back to school.* I wanted to be able to get a better job. I loved the idea of dressing nice for work and having friends who had good jobs. Really, I would have loved to go to college, but my parents had made it very clear that I would never be able to do that. I had never even known anyone who went to college. Who was I to have such a massive dream?

My self-esteem was at an all-time low and I realized that I had little or no self-worth. Who was I to have such a massive dream?

I was so ashamed of myself for dropping out of high school and knew I at least needed to get my GED. *I am not going to be a loser. I made a mistake but I can fix it. I know there is a life better than this. I may never have a great life, but can I at least have a good one? Can I find peace and happiness and wealth somehow? Okay, okay, so that's probably too much to ask for... But could I maybe just feel loved and have some security? God, please help me.*

Creating a New Mindset

Looking back, I should have felt proud of myself. I was learning to take care of my money and make good choices. This situation, though challenging, was actually setting me up for the rest of my life.

On the surface, things were going better than ever. I had the apartment and a better job downtown, but I wasn't content. While at work I saw people who appeared to have what I was looking for, but how did I get there from here? I didn't have a role model and I needed one desperately.

It's like I was living in a bubble. I had no friends who were any better off than I was. I had no one to talk to, no one to share my dreams with (not that I even had a specific dream), no one to tell that I even wanted more. I would ask myself, "Why *can't* I just be happy with what I have? I am making enough to pay my bills. I have a boyfriend who is cute. I am not living with anyone who is causing me harm. It seems like as soon as I get one thing, I want to move on to another. Why?"

I started realizing that it was in my nature to always have my eye on "more." The truth is I had been the same way my entire life, and this would continue to serve me well.

Chapter Four

THE LONG ROAD

I was looking for peace, contentment and happiness but I was on the wrong road. Mark did move in with me... and then came the day I will never forget. I woke up feeling nauseous and called in sick to work – something I never did. As the days went on the nausea continued, and I called my mom to drive me to the doctor. For some reason my dad decided to come with us, but I didn't mind. I just wanted them to figure out why I was sick. Then came the prognosis.

My dad took the news of my pregnancy so hard. Looking at his heartbroken face, I knew I had disgraced him and felt awful. My parents let me know I had two choices.

Number 1: Get married and "give the child a name."

What if Mark was not willing to do that? What if I don't want to marry him? Of course I did want to, I was raised for this, and only this.

Number 2: I could give the baby to them. They would make arrangements for me to go stay at a convent or home for unwed mothers until I had the baby. Then I'd sign the baby over to my parents and they would raise it as their own.

My decision was made quickly when Mark asked me to marry him. Our shotgun wedding happened a few weeks later, with a small reception at my parents'. I was only eighteen and officially a housewife. My self-esteem was so poor I couldn't believe he loved me enough to marry me.

What I remember most about my wedding day was that Chris told me he wouldn't beat me up anymore. I still remember the lump in the pit of my stomach when I met him alone on the landing of the back steps at my reception. Would he kick me in the stomach? Pull me down the stairs by the hair? I was frozen in fear.

He could tell I was petrified. He hugged me and said, "Peggy don't be scared, I promise I won't ever beat you up again."

And he never did.

I soon found I was very comfortable in the role of wife. Again, I had been training for this my whole life. My dad got Mark a better job and this came with lots more money – more than twice the minimum wage. It was a union job with room for advancement, benefits, and regular salary increases. Mark enjoyed his work, took pride in it. I kept working until month eight, and we moved out of the little studio and into a two-bedroom apartment suitable for a family. Mark got his driver's license and we got a car with our tax money; he wrecked it that same week.

I was no longer Peggy, the young women on her own trying to be independent and seeking a better future. I had given up the dream of doing better. No longer was I waiting for Jody Pilcher to ride in and sweep me off my feet again, saving me from this mess

I had made. In the blink of an eye, I had become a wife and soon-to-be mother. How on this earth did I ever believe that marriage or adoption were my only two choices? My parents had forced me to make the decision, which would affect the rest of my life, *five hours* after I found out I was pregnant. I hadn't even thought I might be pregnant before that. I didn't even know anyone my age who'd had a baby. I was still a kid myself.

Why didn't I take charge of my own life? Of course, there were more than the two options presented to me – they were based only on my parents' perception of what I should do, and possibly what they thought was best for them. Their own family was a giant mess, so why did I take advice from them? Youth. Inexperience, I don't know. I do know that I was still young and needed their support even if I didn't live in the house anymore. I knew I couldn't raise a baby without some guidance. I know I was afraid that if I didn't do what they said they might disown me. Here's an FYI for ya: if your kid is too immature to realize that there are more than two choices, she should *not* be getting married. Yes, Mark loved me enough to marry me, and I was happy about that. But, I wonder, what would life have been if I'd had my baby and didn't get married?

Now there were no more dreams of being a fancy bank teller. No more wondering how I could possibly get into college. I was going to stay home and take care of the house and baby, so I set out to be the best house wife and mother I knew how to be. It wasn't easy, since thus far I didn't have any good examples. While I was going through this, my parents were letting my younger siblings drink and smoke pot in the house; it was a free-for-all and I was happy I was out of it. But I wanted so much better for us all.

I had my sweet little Melissa in November; she was the most precious, most beautiful baby ever. Sparkling blue eyes and a smile that lit up the room, well, my whole world. I wanted everything for her. I promised myself and her that no matter what, I would provide stability and love and all the comforts she'd ever need – not just food, shelter, and clothing. Missy walked and talked at a young age. I remember being at the doctor's office with her and another mother said to me, "She's so little tiny. I cannot believe she walks. How much does she weigh?"

Missy replied, "About twenty pounds."

The woman's jaw dropped. I can still see the shock on her face. Yes, that tiny baby could talk too. I believe she was sixteen or eighteen months at the time, and she really was about twenty pounds. I had no idea how exceptional she was. I was not around any other babies, just my own sweet girl.

Mark and I rented a little house for a while, but the neighbors became party buddies for him and I wanted to move away. In fact, we started selling pot for extra money and so he wouldn't have to pay for what he smoked. That was short-lived, it wasn't worth the risk. I would rather have died than jeopardize the baby. Still, he smoked every day, all day, and I smoked a little back then too. By the time I was twenty, I quit; I was sick of being a stoned mom. I wanted to be the best I could be. I knew I could do better. I just didn't know how.

Within a year I knew I had made a huge mistake marrying Mark. He was a total party boy and went out after work a lot, leaving me home with the baby. We were too young to be parents, but while I took the responsibility seriously, he couldn't handle it. At least once a month he'd leave for work Friday morning and be gone the whole weekend. These were the days before cell phones, email and texting; we didn't even have pagers yet. I would just pray that he was okay.

I did eventually go to school to get my GED. It was a year-long course at the college. Fortunately, I passed the pre-tests, got to skip the courses and went straight to the testing. I passed all those tests too and had the certificate in hand in a few months' time. It was with help, though; my family watched the baby for me. Check that off the list! I'd have rather had a high school diploma, but I had the next best thing. I was so happy, and I couldn't believe it was that easy. For so long I had carried the pain of feeling like a complete failure, and it had only taken a couple of months to resolve the issue. This taught me that I should always face my problems instead of being ashamed and hiding secrets in the dark. Let me remember that for next time!

Despite being a wife and mother, it was a lonely life for me. My friends did not have kids, they were at work or school. I did love being with Missy, though. She was smart and I read to her day and night and taught her everything I could. I read about being a mom and watched shows about parents on Oregon Public Broadcasting. Remember, we didn't have the internet back then, so I couldn't just do a quick Google search to get information.

I tried my hardest to keep it together; I kept a nice house and planted flowers in the yard. Mark was still a pothead and drank every weekend, usually at our house because he wasn't drinking age yet. Neither were our friends, so everyone came to our house. We'd have fun until he got too drunk and did something stupid, which happened quite often. He did things like drink and drive or get in fights. He wrecked every car we ever had for the first five or six years. He drove me off a cliff because the breaks were bad, which he knew prior to getting behind the wheel. Another time he fell asleep and hit a guard rail, spinning us around on the highway. That time, the guard rail stopped us from going off the road into the Clackamas River. One time he left to go to the store and came back days later; another time, he tried to get me to swap partners for a night. Oh, yes, life was just great, right off the bat.

One evening we were eating at our little dinner table, with Missy in the high-chair between us, when the phone rang. Imagine my shock when I answered and heard a familiar voice say, "Well you're eighteen..."

I think my heart literally stopped beating. It was Jody – my long-lost love!

"I have a car for you and an apartment," he continued. "I have a good job and I can come and get you next week. I'll bring a friend to ride out with me and we will all drive back. Are you ready for this?"

I didn't answer right away, I just stood there, stuck to the wall by shock and a corded phone and keenly aware that Mark was a few feet away. Mark, my husband, who knew all about Jody. He knew that I had been waiting for him when we first met. Jody was the guy who I'd said I'd drop everything for when he called me. Mark was well aware that included him too; that had been three years earlier, but I had been very clear.

"Jody," I said finally, "I thought you forgot about me. It's been so long. You hadn't called me in a long time. I have a baby girl"

"That's okay, I will take care of her too."

He said it so quickly and earnestly. I believed him.

"Jody, I'm married"

"What? No way! Did you marry Mark Smith?"

"Yes."

"I can't believe you thought I'd forget about you. I can't believe you didn't wait for me. Are you happy?"

"Yes, I am happy," I lied. I hadn't heard from him in so long, how was I supposed to know he'd still call me? Why wouldn't I believe he gave up on us? Why would I think anything different?

"Okay, well, I won't bother you, but I do hope I see you again. I will always love you, Peggy. Goodbye."

"Goodbye, Jody."

He sounded so hurt. I didn't want to hurt him, but he was my past and my future was sitting right here. This was my family. I had made my choice.

Of course Mark had heard every word. He saw the tears streaming from my face. I was clearly heartbroken. There was no hiding it. So I did what I was supposed to do. I assured him I had made my decision to marry him, and I was not going to throw our life away for someone I hadn't heard from in several years. There was no turning back. Mark knew me and knew I was faithful and honest.

Though I didn't talk about Jody again, I would later wonder if that call had an impact on our marriage. I didn't know, but I could guess.

In the meantime, we had bigger problems than the return of an old boyfriend. Mark was a nice guy when he was home; unfortunately, he wasn't home enough. He was still out too often and drank too much. There was always chaos, and it seemed to be getting worse. Bottom line: he didn't have as strong of a desire to be a good parent as I did.

My mom told me that I'd have to wait it out and that he would mature one day.

"Just say your prayers," she'd say, "and hope he will get better."

But what if I didn't want to "wait it out"? When I told my mom I wanted to end the marriage, she reminded me that was not an option. You just don't do that. Nobody in her family had been divorced; it just wasn't acceptable. Marriage is for better or for worse. Besides, Mark was still so young; he was bound to get better with age.

Instead, things went from bad to worse. When Mark turned twenty-one it was a whole new world for him – one that I was even less a part of, one in which he could take his partying out in public. Most Fridays he'd go out right after work, sometimes not coming home until Sunday. Sometimes he spent all the money we needed for bills. I started stashing some of the grocery money, started an emergency fund. I was so unhappy. THIS CAN NOT BE MY LIFE. I wanted to get a job, a career. I wanted something to hope for, to look forward to. Instead, I was holding the home together, just as I had done while growing up. I was good at being a housewife, but I was always missing something. I was smart and I knew it. I would have liked to sell Tupperware or some other evening sales job, but there was no way I could count on Mark to be home for anything like that. I wanted my parents' help but they had kids and jobs and couldn't commit to evenings.

When I was twenty, I started a company called "The Basket Case" and sold wicker items and gift baskets. I found wholesale suppliers and made a few samples and asked my friends if I could bring them to their jobs at lunch. I took orders and did house parties. I made gift baskets for companies, their employees, and their clients before it was "a thing." I made money. Unfortunately, though, it lasted less than a year because life with Mark was too hectic. In fact, it was hell on earth for me.

After that, I tried a series of things to bring me some fulfillment and bring in more money. The first was a job as an assistant apartment manager; we also moved there so we could get our rent for half price. Then I delivered newspapers in the middle of the night. That was short-lived as well. The route took four hours, which meant I had to start by two a.m. to be home in time to get Mark up and ready for work. The problem was, the bar he frequented closed at two-thirty. A couple of nights when he wasn't home in time, I tried to start at three but couldn't get the papers delivered fast enough. Mark's job was more important and when I could rely on his paycheck we had plenty, so I couldn't risk him being fired for coming in late. I also couldn't risk his wrath.

I had a job for a short time at a blueprint company. I recall showing up the second day limping and bruised. It was one of two times that Mark actually hit me. He didn't want me to get a job, but I couldn't hold things together financially without it. Drinking at a bar cost money – lots of it. Once I got the job, he had to go pick up the baby at my parents' house because he got off before me. He didn't like that at all, so we came to an agreement. I would quit and he'd only go out once a week, plus the weekend. Best of all, I could have his check to cash on paydays. He gave up his debit card, and I went to pick up his check at lunch, every other Friday. He had no access to the money unless I gave it to him.

Around that time my dad got hurt at work and my parents asked us to move into their basement and pay rent to help them. We paid them enough to make the entire house payment and paid half the utilities. It was a five-bedroom house and Kelly was the only kid still living at home, so we had privacy. That's when Mark decided to leave us again. Yes, he had taken off before... I think maybe three or four times. This time he moved to California. Despite how bad things were, I was so sad. I had tried so hard and he continued to hurt me. Why couldn't I just move on? Then, after just a few months and before I could make a decision as to what I wanted to do, he came back, got his job back, and we moved out of my parents' house.

While he was gone, I had rekindled my friendship with Kevin, my childhood friend, and his wife, Dawn. This turned out to be a wonderful thing because both he and Mark loved to fish and hunt and do the outdoors. We had lots of fun together when Mark got back. As promised, he came home every night after work. His paycheck was directly deposited and he still didn't have an ATM card. Things were better, but for Mark, something was missing. He was always missing out on something. This time it was a son. He was constantly asking me to have a son. I had a five-year old daughter, an unstable marriage, an alcoholic husband who acted like a boy. I had always planned on having three kids, but I also planned on a happy marriage and a husband who was around. We were getting along great but I was apprehensive. The last thing I needed was for him to tootle off again, leaving me pregnant or with a new baby.

Kevin was a man of honor – a faithful husband, a good provider, and a wonderful friend. When you hang out with great people, it forces you to step up your game and Mark did just that. For several years, things were really good. Eventually I did agree to another child, though the whole pregnancy I was afraid it would be a girl, that he would be disappointed. But ya know, there's a fifty-fifty chance and we got lucky with our son, Tyler. As time went on Kevin and Dawn had two children of their own. I was the babysitter, taking care of all four kids while the three of them went to work. Their family even ate dinner with us two or three times during the week. It was easier like that. Dawn didn't have to go home and cook, and I loved the company after the long days with the kids.

For a while we spent most of our lives together. We were like two families in one. We went to Kevin's parents with them about once a month, and they came to our family gatherings and celebrations too. Oftentimes on the weekends the guys went fishing and Dawn and I found things to do. I was actually settled and content, probably for the first time in my whole life... until that terrible day came.

Mark and Kevin were going on a hunting trip for two weeks. In preparation I bought a food dehydrator and made them smoked salmon and beef jerky and about a hundred dehydrated meals to eat out in the middle of nowhere. Just add water. They headed out in the middle of the night on Friday, after working all week. I remember begging them to get a little sleep and wait until the morning, but they didn't want to waste the time. On Saturday I woke up early and was already sitting in the kitchen when Mark called. It was about seven a.m.

"Peggy," he said, "we were in an accident."

"Where are you?" I still remember the lump in my throat and pit in my stomach.

"I'm at the hospital in Pendleton... Kevin is dead....

I remember falling to the floor and screaming, "Noooooo!"

Dawn, who was staying at our house, came into the kitchen "What happened?"

The phone was still pressed to my ear.

"You have to tell her," Mark was saying.

"I can't tell her THAT!" I cried out loud through my tears. I was sick. I was shocked.

"What happened?!" Dawn asked again, and this time she was crying too.

"There's been a bad accident, Mark is alive but... I'm so sorry... Kevin is dead."

I felt so awful for Dawn – in one instant, her world had capsized. Little did I know that my life had also changed forever. Kevin was my oldest and dearest friend, and we shared a special bond. We were also the glue in our foursome and the strength in our own marriages. We were the reliable ones. The ones with morals and integrity, the faithful ones. Not sure we ever discussed it, but we knew.

With Kevin gone, Mark started drinking again. Dawn went out with him a lot while I stayed home and watched all four kids. They started using cocaine and things went from bad to worse.

One day some months later, I was making the bed when a powerful feeling came over me. I suddenly *knew* that Mark was in love with someone else. I can't explain it, I suddenly knew he had given his heart to another woman. I had never had such a feeling in my life. I waited for his lunch hour and drove to his job.

"Are you in love with someone else?" I asked.

He immediately started to cry. "I'm not in love with her. We haven't slept together. We almost did a couple times, but nothing happened. I promise, nothing has happened. I am glad you know. I'm not okay, I need help. I'm sorry. I'll go to rehab."

And that's what he did, the very next day.

It came as no surprise to me that he needed therapy. The night of the accident he had fallen asleep at the wheel, waking up when he ran into the gravel shoulder. He swerved, and the Jeep started to flip and it rolled over several times. Kevin was thrown from the open passenger window, then the Jeep rolled over him, killing him instantly. Mark never gave me more details, but that was more than enough. I can't imagine what he saw that night, or what he'd continued to see every time he closed his eyes. All I knew was that our lives had fallen apart. We were all broken. Picture The Parthenon with four large stone columns. One fell, that was Kevin. Then Mark and Dawn fell, and I was standing there alone, trying to hold everything together. I constantly had all four kids. I could have gotten someone to watch them and went out too, but I knew that wasn't the answer. The kids needed some stability – everything had changed for them too – and so did I! So I waited for them to come back from grieving and get on with life.

Dawn had newfound freedom and didn't seem to miss Kevin much. It broke my heart. It was so hard – no, I take that back, it was impossible - to believe. How could she move on from such an enormous loss so quickly?

One morning, while Mark was in rehab, it came to me: he was in love with Dawn! Could it be? The day I originally confronted him he wouldn't tell me who it was, and at the time the possibility that it was my best friend didn't occur to me.

Today I was sure God was telling me this, but I had to make sure.

"Hi Dawn," I said when she answered the phone. "I wanted to let you know that Mark told me about the two of you."

The deafening silence confirmed my suspicion.

"He has to come clean in that rehab if it's going to work. So he admitted everything to me."

Dawn started crying.

"I am so sorry, Peggy! Nothing happened. Just kissing. We got too close. You're my best friend. We both love you too much. We're not even going to talk anymore."

I still remember how insulted and hurt I was. That the two of them were "we." "We" got to close. "We" both... How the hell had they become "we"? It was all more than I could handle.

"You can still bring the kids over but I don't want to see you for a while." I refused to let this affect her children; they were going through enough already.

I was sad, really mad at them, and felt utterly stupid, yet, somehow, I understood. We were all so messed up and they had made bad choices. They were drinking and drugging, I reminded myself, and thought, *I'm glad I'm not in their shoes.* I was heartbroken too, but I had allowed myself to feel my pain and work through it.

Everyone grieves in their own way. I knew they were just putting off the grieving process. I wanted to get it out; I didn't need to bury another hurt. Besides, someone needed to be the adult; we had kids to take care of. Naturally, that someone was me.

Now I thought about all I had done, for six months or more, to hold everything together. It had been hard, very hard, way more than I wanted to bear. Knowing the truth about them was the last straw. I was done, I let it crumble to the ground. I lost another battle, probably the war. The truth was, I couldn't save what I had lost. I wasn't strong enough to fight the fight alone anymore. Without Kevin, it was gone. No going back. Things had to get better or we were through.

Once again, I was shocked by how life can completely change so suddenly. In this case, it had been a bit of intuition in the morning and by noon my world had blown up. Suddenly I saw the light. I took off my blinders. Actually, no, that was God.

I didn't know where my life was taking me, or whether Mark would be a part of it. How would he be when he came back from rehab? Would he get back to work and enjoy it? Would they fire him? Would he find a new best friend? Would he get the counseling he needed?

As usual, everything was all about him! I was so sick of him! He had always been an immature jerk but I'd never worried about infidelity. Now I had been betrayed by him in the worst way, and with someone as close as one of my own sisters!

And still the questions continued. Would he and Dawn decide to get together? And what if they had already slept together and were lying about it? Dawn had been sleeping around and AIDS was rampant at the time – did I have to worry about that too?

This led me to re-examine everything about my life. *Why do I rely on Mark? He's unreliable. I don't have to stay home because he says so. I don't have to be a housewife because my parents say so. What am I doing here? This is my life. I am twenty-six years old and I've done nothing for myself.*

I need to figure out what I want. I refuse to count on him anymore.

I knew in my heart that what happened next would make or break things for us.

When the holidays came, he'd been out of drug rehab five or six months. He'd made it through without a drink. He had a newfound life at AA. Call me crazy, but in a weird way I was jealous of that life. On New Year's Eve we hosted an alcohol-free party at our house. Some old friends and some from AA. When our guests left shortly after midnight, he was sitting on the couch. I cleaned up a bit, pulled out my notebook, plopped on the couch next to him, and enthusiastically said, "Let's make some goals for 1990!" I was so happy that he stayed sober for the holiday season. I had hopes that things could work out after all.

His response stunned me like nothing I'd ever heard before.

"I've been doing a lot of thinking about my future and it doesn't look bright. Not with you, Peggy. I don't think I will get anywhere as long as I'm with you."

I may have been speechless, but I had a million thoughts running around in my head. I had held this ridiculous marriage together for years. I was the strong one. I fixed up the house and took care of the kids. It was me that was there every time he was sick or down on himself. It was my parents who helped us get the house, my dad who'd gotten him his job. I was the one who scrimped and saved money so that when the paycheck got blown on drugs we never missed a house payment. Not one. Not ever. I was the one who made sure we weren't left without water or electricity. I was the one who made dinner every night and got up at five am. to make his breakfast and lunch and then woke him up for work. I was the responsible one.

It's funny. I had prayed so many times that he would stay, and I would thank God even more that he finally left me.

Yes, he had left before, but this time was different because I couldn't blame it on the drugs or alcohol, or his frame of mind. It wasn't after a big disagreement or fight. He just told me he'd had enough of me. I couldn't blame anyone else or anything else anymore; I had run out of excuses for him.

"Okay," I said, "If you want to go, go. But if you leave me this time I swear I will not take you back, so make sure it's what you want. This will be the end of our relationship. The end of our family."

He assured me that he'd been thinking about it for months.

"Well, I just spent all the money on Christmas," I said, all business as I took out my calendar. "You can't leave for the next two paychecks. You'll need money and I will need money. It looks like you can move on February tenth."

He agreed. The next day, by his choice, he moved downstairs into his den, where he slept the last weeks of our marriage. Despite my bravado, I secretly prayed every night that he would change his mind. He did not. During those weeks, I changed.

He had been dragging us down for the past ten years, while I kept our heads above water. Now *he* had places to go? Really?

I started telling myself that I could have a better life. That I would have freedom to be myself. I did not know who I was, or how to find that beautiful person hiding inside me, but I would.

I was determined to show Mr. Smith that I was not holding him back. Truth is, he was holding me back! Somehow, I not only believed it; for once, I actually saw the truth. I *knew* it!

I also knew the breakup of my marriage was the best thing for me, but it was still the hardest thing I'd ever been through. Aside from the short period in my own apartment, I had never supported myself. The longest I'd even held a job was a year and half when I worked at McDonalds. I had no self-worth or confidence in my abilities. I had put all my eggs in Mark's basket and after all these years, I was completely beaten down.

I thought about all I had put up with during our marriage. As mentioned, there were "only" a few times he actually beat on me, but he destroyed many things – furniture, walls he punched holes in and doors he kicked through. I recalled the Thanksgiving he'd gotten mad at something while we were at my parents' house – he was drunk, of course – and went nuts. When I wouldn't give him the keys he left for home on foot, about seven or eight miles away. I went home and parked my car behind his in the driveway so he couldn't get behind the wheel drunk. I had just finished putting the kids to bed when he came in, still mad about who knows what.

He yelled at me from the front door. "Move your car out of my way."

"No, Mark, don't drink and drive. What are you mad about?"

"Get your car out of my way!"

"No, I'm not going to let you be stupid. Just come in and go to bed."

He went out to his Jeep and rammed my car over and over and over until he pushed it into the street, damaging both cars, he then tore out of the driveway and into the night. All the neighbors had heard the crashing sounds and ran outside to witness the spectacle. My Mustang was pretty wrecked, just one more car he had destroyed, and I couldn't even file an insurance claim. He had destroyed so many cars that in 1988 we were paying three hundred and eighty-six dollars a month for our car insurance. More than thirty years later, I still don't pay half that.

He also put me down all the time – I wasn't that smart, not that pretty. He actually said my sister and I could sink a ship if we got on it together. At the time we each wore a size seven or eight; I probably weighed one hundred and thirty pounds and had a six-week-old baby. I was so afraid to gain weight. I was always afraid he'd find someone else and leave me and not come back. I can't believe I lived like that. I knew I needed to make a plan for independence, but I never did.

I let him make me feel so small. After being raised the way I was, I didn't think I should leave him. I guess I believed I didn't deserve any better. All I know is that finally, I'd had all I could take. I allowed myself to see the truth – the wreckage. I knew I had had enough. Finally!

Chapter Five

YES, YOU CAN!

"*B*egin with the end in mind" is one of my favorite credos to live by.

I cried when Mark left, just shy of ten years of marriage, and a million more tears followed. Yet I was bound and determined to move on. Meeting men was of no interest to me, all that mattered was supporting my kids and creating a better life for all of us. I was not sure how or what I was going to do, so for now I just focused on "onward and upward." I had always imagined a life where I felt peace and security, but except for the few months I lived on my own at seventeen, I'd never had that. Now I wanted it back.

Instead, I ended up on welfare for almost a year. It was the worst time of my life. I never told my dad because I didn't want him to lose respect for me. He didn't believe in hand-outs and that went for me too. But after Mark stopped paying support I went to the welfare office to get insurance and they offered me cash as well.

Turned out Mark did change his mind about leaving, and he threatened several times that if I didn't take him back he would quit his job and move away.

"We'll see how high and mighty you are without my support and alimony," he'd say.

Soon he started drinking again, and it wasn't long before he decided he would no longer help us out. It was disgusting, but yes, he stooped that low. Melissa, then eight years old, was especially heartbroken. She was daddy's girl. All those years of hiding his shortcomings was going out the window. He had abandoned us and I was living each month on under four hundred dollars. We had more than that each week when I was married. But we managed. I moved from my beautiful home to a friend's attic. I set it up into a living room and bedroom for the kids. I was grateful.

During that awful time in my life one of the most remarkable things happened. The summer before Mark and I split up, my friend Brad got married. Mark was uncomfortable at the reception; it was the first occasion he had to be around alcohol without drinking and he didn't know how to enjoy himself. He didn't mingle or dance. He just sat at the table like a lump on a log and I, the ever-dutiful wife, felt obligated to stay by his side. I wasn't too happy about this. I didn't need to drink to have fun. I wanted to talk and laugh and dance with my friends. Instead, I stayed close and enjoyed the celebration as best I could. Fortunately, a guy came and sat at our table with us. He was alone and he and I started talking. His name was Jerry and I knew it well, as he had grown up with the groom and my good friend Otto and they'd told me all about him. That day Jerry and I became fast friends, which of course annoyed Mark even more. He was so busy feeling sorry for himself that he didn't want to get to know Jerry. He didn't want anyone sitting there with us. He didn't want me to enjoy myself either. Soon, he wanted to leave.

I pleaded my case, saying everything from, "They haven't even cut the cake yet" to "They've been planning this wedding for months" and "I haven't even gotten to dance yet."

Mark didn't care. "Get the kids, let's go!"

Jerry said, "Mark, I'd be happy to bring Peggy home since the party's just getting started. This way you can leave and she can stay and dance."

There was no chance I was going to get to stay. No way. I got the kids and went home with Mark. I remember how bad I wanted to just get back in the car and go back to the party. All my friends were there. It was going to be so much fun. I realized that if he was going to stay sober this would probably be my new life.

Just a few months earlier the situation would have looked something like this:

We would have been at the party late, with me saying that we needed to go home because the kids were tired. He would've said, "Okay, okay, soon. Just let me finish this drink." But that one would lead to one more drink and then another and another. He may or may not have left with me. He may or may not have come home at all that night. He may not have come home at all the weekend! Boy, had things changed. Now I couldn't even have a dance or two at a friend's wedding reception. He was the alcoholic, but whether he was drinking or not, I had the problem.

Then Came Jerry

Mark moved out on February eleventh, right before my birthday, which is on Valentine's Day. I've always loved that day. People remember. It is a day that has made me feel really loved. That year, newly separated, I dreaded being alone. Little did I know that one of the best things in life was about to happen to me. It was a God thing.

The night before my birthday, my phone rang.

"Hi, Peggy, this is Jerry, I met you at Brad and May's wedding. Do you remember me?"

"Yes, of course I do. How are you?"

"I'm okay. Nina and I broke up and I heard you and Mark split up recently. I am so sorry to hear about that. Are you doing okay"?

"I will be fine," I assured him. I meant every word.

"Well, I was wondering if you would be my Valentine this year? I'd like to take you to dinner if you're available."

"What do you mean, Valentine?"

"Not a real date!" he assured me. I could hear the laughter in his voice. "I'm not trying to hit on you. I know you were with Mark for a long time. No sense in both of us staying home on Valentine's Day alone, right?"

"Oh, okay, then. I'd love to."

"Great! I'll pick you up at six. See you tomorrow."

I hung up the phone with a big giant smile on my face, unable to believe this was happening. He was a handsome guy with a great job and a sports car. I could not believe he would even want to be seen with me. Oh my gosh. Suddenly my new life wasn't looking nearly as bad as it had been. I had a Valentine, and a cute one at that!

Again, I knew it wasn't a date; nor did I want it to be. I was convinced I was unattractive. I had been told nobody would ever love me again, and I believed it, so this invitation meant the world to me.

The next evening my parents babysat my kids. Jerry showed up there promptly at six with flowers. So sweet. We went out for

Chinese food and then to a club for a little dancing. He let me know it would be an early evening because he started work at six a.m. We had one drink as we sat and talked. He was such a nice guy. He encouraged me, he told me he had known about me for years through our friends and that I was the strong one. I was the good one. I could do anything I wanted with my new life. I didn't have to listen to Mark putting me down anymore. I didn't need to believe what he said about me. It was time to try to let all that go.

This was a giant boost of confidence. I still don't know how could Jerry have known my heart, or how he could have seen me like that. How did he know all the right things to say? He didn't want anything from me, so he wasn't just telling me what I wanted to hear in order to take advantage of my broken spirit.

During dinner someone came around selling roses and taking polaroid pictures. "Would you like a rose and picture to commemorate your date tonight?" they asked.

I said, "No thanks," but Jerry chimed in.

"What? Of course, we do!"

He gave me the picture and the flower and said, "You need to remember this day. This is a great day, Peggy; this is the first day of your new life. You're going to do great. You've got what it takes."

I really wanted to believe him. He was just a genuine nice guy. Heartwarming.

He took me home at about eleven. It had been a great night... until I got up the steps of the porch and saw Mark sprawled out across the doorway. He had been sleeping but woke up as I approached.

"What are you doing here?" I asked.

"Where have you been?" Mark questioned me, as if he had a right.

"That is none of your business, Mark. Now go home."

"I can't believe you are already out on a date with this guy."

"It's not your business," I repeated, "I will go out with whoever I want. Now go home and leave me alone."

He left quietly and peacefully. I didn't even feel bad for him. It was a new day for me. I was getting stronger by the day. I also knew that if Jerry hadn't asked me out, if I had been sitting home alone with my broken heart, I would have let Mark in. He probably would have suggested a family dinner or something. I don't know where I'd be right now and thank God I never will.

God puts people in your life at the right time. For me, that was Jerry. He sat next to me at a wedding while he waited for his date and that was a miracle. It led to our Valentine's "unofficial date." Be open to miracles, they happen all the time. We both went to the same wedding, we were strangers. But we were destined to meet. That day, that date, changed my life. I just needed someone to tell me something good about me that I was able to hear and believe. He told me things I had never heard before.

Jerry and I are friends to this day – he is actually married to my best friend Shelly – and I love him and see him often. I still believe he saved my life that night all those years ago, and I am forever grateful.

Another game-changer happened that first week. I went to get a haircut, my eyes still red from crying about Mark and wondering how to make my way in life. Dolores, my hairdresser, encouraged me to go to school and learn to cut hair. She promised me a job when I got out. She was hoping to get pregnant and wouldn't want to work full time after the baby came. I'd be perfect, she said; I had the gift of gab and liked people. I loved the idea. I had been looking for a way out, a way to find new friends and new experiences, and this certainly seemed like it might be that way. Yet there was also a voice in my head, telling me I was too ugly to be a hairdresser; they were always so cute and stylish. In the end, my desire for a better life won out, and with Delores' help I found all the information for the school and financial aid. A week later, I was enrolled. I had a plan!

Imagine the life you want; *see* that future unfolding for you. When I want to bring something into my reality, I contemplate, I pray, and step out in faith.

Jon

Jerry's kindness that night had been a turning point for me, evidence that there were men out there who would lift me up rather than drag me down. As it turned out, however, my challenges were far from over. In fact, my first boyfriend after Mark was even worse than Mark. I guess I was just so happy to find a guy who was interested in me that I was willing to overlook a few things.

Jon was Romanian, and as I had never known a European man he seemed pretty exotic. He was handsome and had a good job; he took me out to nice dinners and events. He was a sharp dresser and a good dancer. He was so much fun and a breath of fresh air. He didn't make a lot of demands on me, he let my kids come first. He bought me nice dresses and nice shoes and taught me to treat myself like a lady. I loved it! I had been a tomboy, a hard worker my whole life, so this was a whole new world for me. Between meeting him and making the decision to go to beauty school, it seemed my new life was coming together.

In many ways, Jon was indeed different from the guys I'd always known. He was also, it turned out, chauvinistic, jealous and possessive. He didn't trust women, including me, and the closer we got the more jealous he became. He said he never wanted to get married again, so I couldn't figure out what the possessiveness was all about. He contradicted himself but I didn't have the confidence to call him out on it, plus I was having fun for the first time in a long time. I hadn't had much experience with men, having had only two boyfriends, one of which I married, and at twenty-seven I was new to the world of adult dating. I had no idea how to spot a red flag and run.

I decided I would make him trust women again. I thought, *I am loyal. He'll see. I am so trustworthy he won't have to worry.* But Jon said he wanted no part of a commitment, so my girlfriends encouraged me to spend some time going out on dates with other guys too. I took their advice and decided I would be open to playing the field. Why not? Why be closed off to other guys when Jon didn't want anything serious? I was beginning to enjoy my new life. I had been in a little tiny world, and now there were infinite possibilities, so many interesting people, and I was drinking it up.

Beauty school was easy for me and I liked it. I went to the thrift store and got "hairdresser clothes" – skirts, blouses, jackets, shoes, all different styles. I was learning what suited me and I was having fun doing it. I had worn jeans and tee-shirts my whole life. I never bought cute stuff for myself. I had been blessed with friends who gave me clothes over the years, so I never looked bad or raggedy, and besides, I never went anywhere anyway. I had a haircut once or twice a year. I wore cheap makeup, which didn't matter to me. I didn't wear much anyway, just eyeliner and lip gloss. I didn't have any idea what I was missing out on, so I didn't miss anything. I spent all the money I ever had on Mark's never-ending hobbies and the rest of it went for stuff for the kids. There really wasn't much left for me.

I didn't mind all those years of putting them first. I wanted my kids to have things. I had vowed they would have as much as I could give them. I would not allow them to be raised with nothing like I was. But once I started dressing girly and fixing my hair, I must say I looked better. Prettier, maybe. I felt better about myself; I gained confidence. Men started talking to me – lots of them. It felt like they were coming out of the woodwork, probably because I wore an ear-to-ear grin most of the time. It was exciting and amazing. At last, a brand new me. I liked her.

I went out with a few guys I met in downtown Portland, where my school was, but Friday and Saturday were the nights I loved; they were the nights to go out. I had school at eight-thirty Saturday morning and church on Sunday at nine a.m., so I never got to sleep in. That first year, I usually went out one night or the other. My mom used to tell us, "If you're gonna dance, you have to pay the fiddler," and I did!

I know I went out too much. My kids were young and needed me. Their dad had left them too; I should have spent my time with them. They were used to my being home twenty-four-seven, now I was going to school five days a week from eight-thirty to five-thirty, working at a frame shop for two or three hours a few nights a week, and going out with friends whenever I could. It took me a long time to forgive myself for not being home more, but for the first time in my life I was putting myself at the top of the list. And I was having so much fun meeting all these new people and dancing the nights away! That was how I met Jon.

He always had lots of the girls hanging around him, but week after week, he'd send a drink over to me and ask me to dance. At first, I kept my distance. I liked him, but I was scared. I wouldn't dream of going out with a stranger. A lot of people would go out to eat after they danced all night but that was way out of my comfort zone and, like I said, I always had school or church the following morning.

Then, one Saturday, Jon showed up at my school; he didn't want a haircut, just a wash and dry. I'm sure he didn't trust me to cut his hair. I was new to barbering and he knew it. He asked me to go to lunch and I said yes. I was happy he still liked me in the daylight. That bar was dark and people look better when you are drinking, so we'd made it past that hurdle. We laughed and talked and next thing you knew we had a plan for dinner that night. After that I started meeting him once a week at the club, but now we would sit and dance mostly with each other, rather than with others like we had before. After a while he even started going to bingo with me to meet my mom, my aunt, and a few friends. They all liked him. He was a ladies' man and we were all enamored, but again, he wanted no commitment so I let him know I was going to see other guys.

Marty, who I met at school, was the total opposite of Jon. For one, he was a bowler, not a dancer. He was also ruggedly handsome and strong, a "man's man," and a kind soul, not a player. Marty was going to barber college so he could take over his dad's barber shop, and he was great at cutting hair. He was shy but well-liked, and loyal – you could see it in his eyes. Most importantly, he was the settling-down type and that was just what I needed. I went after him, and he fell for me.

Now, this was really a crazy, and a new thing for me. Jon went to visit his family and when he returned from Romania, he still wanted to date me. He knew I was seeing Marty. Marty loved me and wanted a commitment. He didn't know Jon was still in the picture, and I felt like I could justify the lie because I was only seeing Jon "a little bit." It was ending. Going nowhere. I figured Jon would go back to Romania again and that would be the end of us, so why muddy the waters? Jon was a challenge; I wanted him to love me, but he refused. He got an apartment near me, and he would call to see how I was doing and if I'd meet him to dance on the weekends. Sometimes I did; sometimes I was with Marty.

Jon would say it was cruel of me to see someone else before he left, but I stood my ground. "I am not going to sit around waiting for you to come back when you don't love me and we have no commitment." I saw him or talked to him about once a week and went out even less than that. I was working on moving on.

About a week before his trip to Europe, Jon finally relented. At his request, I stopped by his apartment one day after work; I figured I would just see what he wanted and head home because Marty was coming over that evening. Imagine my surprise when Jon then started telling me how much he loved me! He didn't want to, but he did.

"I am so sorry," I said, "but I don't have time for this right now. I have to go home. My kids are waiting, my parents are expecting me; so is Marty. I will have to talk to you about it later."

Then Jon then started to cry! He was leaving for Romania soon and he didn't want to lose me. He realized I was his only reason to come back to the US. Now he wanted a commitment.

I was completely torn. Jon said he loved me, but what about poor Marty? He was steady Eddie. He was true blue. He was everything I was looking for. He was everything I needed. And Jon, he was just a challenge, wasn't he? I just really wanted him to love me because he wouldn't, right? I couldn't throw Marty aside for this guy, could I? Why would I? Marty would never let me see another guy. There was no way, he was a one-woman man and would only accept a one-man woman. What was wrong with me? How had I let myself get into this? I didn't want to hurt anyone, but after all this time, Jon loved me! He really loved me. I knew it! I knew it! How could he not?

After dinner, Marty came over and we walked the kids to my parents, who lived in the same apartment complex. Both liked Marty, especially my dad. My mom knew I was seeing two men and she did not approve, mostly because Marty didn't know. We visited with them for a while, then I asked if the kids could stay in their guest room. They agreed, and Marty and I held hands as we walked back to my apartment. He said he was glad we were alone because he wanted to talk. As soon as we got inside, he asked me to marry him.

What? Wait, what the hell is going on?

"Marty, I am so sorry. I was planning to break up with you." I was overwhelmed, my eyes were full of tears, and I could see how hurt he was. I had broken someone's heart and I knew first- hand how bad that felt.

Marty wasn't going to let things go that easily.

"Why, how could you? We get along great. I'll take care of you guys. I'll be a great dad for Tyler. I thought you loved me. How could you do this? I didn't see this coming at all. You are making a mistake; I will take care of you. I will love you and the kids forever. You won't have to hope for child support from that deadbeat dad of theirs, I'll adopt them and take them in as my own. Why would you do this to us? What happened, what has changed?"

Oh my gosh, was I really doing this? That's when I finally came clean: I was getting back together with Jon. He needed me.

When he heard that, Marty's sadness turned to anger. The last thing he said was, "You deserve each other," and then he walked out the door. I never saw him again. Actually, I take that back. I think I saw him about five years later at a big festival, with a wife and twins in a stroller. I looked right at him; our eyes met for a few seconds. I smiled, and though he didn't acknowledge me I think it was him. I hope it was... I want to believe he found happiness with a good wife.

After he left that night, I was upset and so sad. I had just broken up with a great guy, and for what? For a guy who had refused to commit to me until an hour ago. What was I thinking? Why was I knowingly choosing the wrong guy? Why did I just let the right guy go? I couldn't stop myself. I grabbed my jacket because it was raining and walked the six hundred steps to Jon's apartment. When I got there, I told him I wasn't going to stay long. I just really wanted to take a bath. He had a much nicer bathtub than I did; it was big and deep, and mine was a little apartment tub/shower combination.

I filled up a bubble bath and while I was soaking, he came in and kneeled next to the bubble-filled tub and said, "I love you. Will you marry me?"

Shocked, I somehow managed to say yes, and he put a beautiful ring on my finger.

How had this happened? Why did I say yes? That morning I had planned on staying with Marty and letting Jon down gently when he went back to Romania. Now I was marrying him? My life was out of control and I needed to figure it out.

When I finished my bath, I got dressed, told Jon I didn't feel good, and went home. It was the truth! I wasn't happy like a woman who was just engaged. I was sick to my stomach. While I was walking home on that dark rainy night, I put the ring in my pocket, picked up my kids from my parents, went home, went to bed, and cried myself to sleep. Dear God, what had I done?

I knew I needed help, but I had no idea where to find it. I didn't even have the words to express the disappointment I had in myself. *At least he's leaving next week and I will be able to sort this out while he's gone.* (That still sounds ridiculous, even thirty years later.)

Jon and I decided we would get married when he returned to the States in six months. We were going to buy a house together, and I could look for it, and plan a wedding, while he was gone. After a few weeks I realized I didn't miss him at all. I hadn't been seeing him much anyway. I had recently graduated from beauty school and thankfully, Delores had kept her word and hired me as soon as I was licensed. I loved working at the salon; it was fun, I was making money, and Delores was teaching me the things I didn't learn in school.

It worked for both of us. Delores had just found out she was pregnant and had morning sickness, so she was happy that I could do walk-ins and answer the phone for her. Also, I was already bringing in new business. I had a ton of friends and neighbors and I even had two or three clients come from my school downtown for haircuts. The school where I had been working charged three dollars for haircuts, and now I was charging twelve dollars for men and fifteen dollars for women. It didn't make sense that people would travel thirty minutes and pay three or four times the normal amount to go to me, but they did and it felt great. Right off the bat I was making enough money to pay my bills and have just a bit left over. I never thought I'd be able to quit the part-time job at the frame shop, but

I did. If they were behind, I still worked Mondays when the salon was closed. I owed them the favor for giving me a job when I needed one, and I could always use the money.

Art Remlinger

One of the customers who came out to my new place of business was an eighty-two-year-old man named Art Remlinger. Art and I had formed a friendship while I was in beauty school. He lived about ten blocks away, and one day he came in for a three-dollar haircut and by chance (or miracle) was assigned to me. Delores had been right when she said I was blessed with the gift of gab; I could talk to most people without effort, and Art was no different. He opened up to me, saying that Christine, his wife of sixty years, had died just a few weeks earlier on Christmas day, and I'm certain I told him of my recent divorce. When he checked out, he left me a *twenty-dollar* tip – unheard of on a three-dollar haircut! Thank you, God, for always blessing me.

Art came back the next month and asked for me; then two or three weeks later for a trim. When he came back the next week, I understood that he was lonesome without Christine and just wanted the company. I told him he didn't need a trim, and that I had two fifteen-minute breaks and a lunch every day. I studied on my lunch, but I could have coffee on my morning break. He didn't have to pay for a haircut he didn't need; I would be his friend.

For a few weeks he came most days and we went across the street and had coffee and chatted. He had so many stories to tell. He'd made his money in the stock market; he had worked for the pony express and had a job in an office that sent telegrams. It was amazing to me that he had lived through two world wars and the Depression.

One day while we were at coffee he asked if I would consider moving into the spare bedroom of his apartment and cooking and cleaning for him. He knew I was living in a friend's attic with my two kids. I wondered what the apartment looked like. After all, this was a man who went to a barber college for a three-dollar haircut.

"I am lonesome there by myself and I need help," he said. "You would grocery shop and cook, I will pay for all the groceries. You'd have to keep the house dusted and tidy. I am not a messy man, but I don't like to deep clean and I can't even see the dust." He laughed.

I wouldn't have to pay rent, plus he'd pay me five hundred dollars a month – a huge amount for me. Still, it was a big decision, and I asked him if it was okay if I brought my mom and dad when I come to see the place.

Art said yes and we made the plan. I got his address and decided to go by on my lunch to check it out before I told my parents about it. If it wasn't in a decent part of town or it looked rundown, I wouldn't bother.

I also wondered how he would be with my kids. Tyler was hyper – how would he live with this old man? I started weighing things in my mind: I wouldn't have to pay rent out of the tiny bit of money I had; Art would buy the food for all of us, and fill my car with gas since I'd have to drive the kids back and forth over the bridge. I liked to cook and I was always cleaning anyway...

I called my dad and told him what happened, then on my lunch break I walked the ten blocks to the apartment. Oh, my gosh! Was this really happening? He lived in the Portland Plaza – a round high-rise made of glass with a view of the mountains. A river view and you could see every bridge heading into downtown Portland. I had often wondered about the people who lived in that beautiful building and how they got so lucky. Could it be that I was going to move from an attic into a beautiful condo? I went back to school and called my dad and told him where it was.

At five-forty-five I met my parents out front. As soon as we went into the lobby I felt out of place. I had never been in such a nice apartment before! A doorman greeted us immediately and was very pleasant. I am certain he knew none of us belonged there, but was nice to us just the same.

I could hear the nervousness in my voice as I told him my name and that Art Remlinger was expecting us. He called Art, who instructed him to send us up.

"Do you know where his apartment is?"

No, I didn't.

"He is number twenty-four twenty-five. You can take this elevator up to the twenty-fourth floor and turn left. It will be on your right."

Shocked, I thanked him and we boarded the elevator. Oh my gosh, I thought, looking at the buttons, there were only twenty-five floors in the whole building! I would later learn that there were a couple penthouses and gardens up there. As we ascended, I was smiling from ear-to-ear but my mind was racing. How could this be happening to us? Who cared if I had to share a room with the kids? I wouldn't change their school and babysitter until I knew this would work long- term. I was graduating in less than a year anyway so we'd have to see what happened over the next few months. But in the meantime, amazing.

When the elevator door opened, Art was there to greet us. He was very happy to see me, and I was happy to see how nice this apartment was. A panoramic view for miles. Spectacular. We went over his expectations, which were very few: cooking, shopping, and light cleaning; I was free to come and go as long as I ate dinner with him. I asked about the floor-to-ceiling windows. "I can't clean those," I told him honestly. He laughed and said he hired someone to do the windows a few times a year. He was also willing to continue paying his housekeeper once a week to do the bathrooms and other dirty things. "You get your own parking spot down in the garage," he added.

I was going to make five hundred a month to cook and keep this guy company at dinner and I wouldn't have to live in an attic anymore. Deal. I had hit the jackpot just because I was kind to someone who needed a friend. God was so good to me! I honestly couldn't believe this was real, so there was one last thing I needed to check...

"I am not your girlfriend or anything like that, right?"

He laughed again. "That's right. I am an old man and I just really need company. I am lonely here all by myself without Christine."

After that it was just a matter of hammering out the schedule. I told him I had school Tuesday through Saturday, then I had to go pick up the kids. Sundays I need off because I taught Sunday school and went to church, then spent the rest of the day with my parents and the rest of my family; I would make enough on Saturday night so he had leftovers or leave something else to eat while I was gone. On Mondays I would take him to run errands or visit, or shop or whatever else he needed to do. Then I reiterated that I was not his girlfriend.

"Oh, I know you're not." he chuckled again.

The kids and I moved in right away. I was so grateful to my good friends Otto and Cindy for giving me a place to live, as well as companionship and love, in my time of need, but boy was I happy to be out of their attic!

As it turned out, the arrangement only lasted a few months. It was a beautiful place to live and we had a pretty big room, but there was no space to play. Plus, I was constantly trying to make sure that Tyler didn't break anything, and though Art was always nice and never complained about him, it was no place for kids.

I told Art we were moving out but I would come straight over after school and make dinner and eat with him; I would also come over for the whole day on Mondays. He said he would continue to pay me the five hundred a month. I had saved every penny I earned and was able to get an apartment where my parents lived as the managers. To my surprise, Art paid my first, last, and deposit for me!

For the rest of the time I was in school I continued to see him every day, except Sunday, but it wasn't working for him. He was still lonely. I have to admit I did rush the dinner, then I started cooking a bunch on the weekends so I could just go heat it up and have a few extra minutes to visit. The funny thing is, two or three days a week Art would cook dinner for me. I felt guilty because I knew I was taking advantage and not giving him the companionship he needed. He was constantly trying to spend his money on me, offering me cars and clothes and trips. He even surprised me with a trip to London on the Concord! Oh man, I wanted to go, but didn't. I didn't want to use him for his money or lead him on, so I asked my sister to go with him and she did. Still, pretty soon he started asking me to marry him every time I saw him.

"I will buy a house for you that has a yard and an apartment. We can live wherever you want Peggy."

"But Art, you love this place; I don't think you should sell it. It is so beautiful. It is perfect for you."

"Well, then, let's get married. I will give you this condo as a wedding gift and when Tyler is grown and I am gone you can live here and enjoy it."

"Art, I can't even afford the association fees and taxes."

"I will prepay the fees for five years and give you two hundred and fifty thousand in cash on our wedding day. You can invest that money because I will pay for everything for you and your kids until the day I die. I can't have sex anymore, so you don't have to worry about that. I will leave you alone." He said that last part with a grin.

I thought for a moment and asked, "Do I have to sleep in the same bed with you?"

"Of course, you'd be my wife."

I had to be honest with him. "Art, I can't marry you. I wouldn't be faithful; I would be looking at other men, wondering. Besides, I believe God has a great husband for me and I will not meet him if I am married to you. This isn't a marriage; this is a business deal. I would be doing it for the money. I want God's blessing. Art, we are just friends, and my taking care of you is a job."

"But two-hundred and fifty thousand dollars...?" he asked.

Believe me, I was tempted!

"No," I laughed, "and don't be crazy. Let's try to find someone who will love you and be a good wife to you. Someone your own age. You are happy downtown; you can walk to all your favorite places and I will take you everywhere else. If you want to fire me, fire me. You don't have to pay the five hundred a month and I will still come to visit you on Mondays. I will be earning more money soon anyway."

Well, he did fire me and I went back to my part-time job at the frame shop. I still spent my Mondays with Art and he never quit bugging me to marry him.

My mom didn't quit bugging me to marry him either. "Don't be silly Peggy." she said. "You married once for love. That got you nowhere. Take what you can get. You'll still be young when he dies. You can get married for love again later, with lots of money in the bank."

"Mom! Really? Well, where is God in that? What does God want for me?" I didn't know, but I was sure it wasn't to get married and wait for the old man to die.

In the meantime, God was blessing me with lots of customers and referrals. I was great at men's haircuts and busy all day, taking all the guys who didn't ask for Delores specifically. I was even on TV, cutting a marine sergeant's "high and tight" cut for a tv commercial the school was doing. I had much less experience and confidence with women – I had, after all, gone to barber school – but Dolores was a good teacher and I got plenty of on-the-job training. Everything was going great, but there was still something hanging over my head: my engagement to Jon.

I knew I didn't want to marry him. He had done and said some crazy stuff before he left for Romania. Once he was gone, I saw how wrong it was. He was not for me. I started looking back at the relationship more with my head and less with my heart. I realized the more he pushed me away, the more I had wanted his love. But that wasn't because I loved him so much, it was because I didn't want to face the rejection. I had already been rejected by Mark – not to mention the years when my brother Chris treated me so badly – and I didn't want to go through that again. But guess what? Not everyone is going to love you! They just aren't! I was beginning to see that it was their loss. Plus, even if someone does love you it doesn't mean they are right for you. You don't have to love them back. I had learned I would rather be single than with the wrong person. *I am not afraid to be alone,* I told myself, until I believed it. It had been an adjustment, but I was getting stronger. Besides, I had kids who were counting on me to make good decisions, and I wasn't going to let them down.

My mind was made up; I would have to break the news to him when he returned. At least he had money saved, and he would need it to get his own place. We had planned to get married right away and live together in my apartment while we looked for a home to buy. He had put his furniture in storage, so he'd have what he needed. I figured I could let him stay with us for a few days while he found something, and that would be that.

Guys, if you don't like where you are at, do something! Grumbling, complaining, and living in regret will only keep you stuck. See what needs to change and take one step, and then another and then another. As far as I know, it's the only way out. Look at the problem honestly, see what can be done, and make a plan. Then do it.

I could almost hear God saying, *Change is coming, Change IS coming, CHANGE IS COMING.*

It was coming, alright. I had been working for Dolores for about six months when she announced she was selling the salon. That was her last month there. She had found out that her baby was autistic and she needed to be home with her. Though I understood her decision, I was devastated. I was finally doing well!

"Who is buying it?" I asked.

She didn't know yet, just that she was going to put it up for sale. Her lease was up in a month so if it didn't sell by then she would have to shut the doors. I wondered, could I buy it? I started asking her for details: what the rent, utilities, insurance, and licenses cost. What did it take to own a salon? I have no idea why or how I even thought that I could own a business. I knew absolutely nothing about it. I just knew I was doing well and I didn't want to move. I could make a go of it there. I just knew it.

I had never asked Art for anything before, but when he came in for his next haircut I talked to him. I wondered if he thought it was a good deal and if I could be successful... and if he would loan me the money if the numbers worked. Delores wanted five thousand dollars.

"I don't know how much I can pay you per month," I said, "So, I don't know how long it would take me to pay you back. But I will pay you back."

I hadn't even considered interest, and he explained to me why when getting a loan you have to have a detailed business plan, in writing, that includes projections for the future. I was surprised that he wanted to charge me interest, but I didn't mind. Business is business. As long as I could afford the payment, I would make the deal. As I cut his hair we talked about the reasons why I wanted it.

I was making money. The salon had been here for quite a while so lots of people walked in. I knew I could be successful running my own business, I told him, I was already envisioning what I would do with it. He then went in the back and talked to Dolores while I did my next client.

After speaking with him Dolores left the salon, and left me wondering what Art would say. I just hoped she had given him enough information to justify taking a risk on me. When I was done with the customer, I sat down in the waiting area with him. He told me to go home after work and write out a budget for home and another one for the salon.

"Be thorough," he advised, "You need to know what you are getting into before you take a leap." I promised I would. First, I needed to talk to Dolores and find out what her expenses were. I wanted to show him I could do a business plan, even though I had never written one in my life. Then I would show him my budget and what I'd been doing at home with my money.

I did call him a few times that night with some questions. I didn't want to disappoint him or fall short of his expectations. I went to the bank and got a printout to show him I had a few thousand dollars I had saved from the money I earned from him.

He came back in the next day; we went to coffee and I showed him both of my budgets and the business plan. I was going to paint and get new decorations to make the salon more modern. I would rent out chairs to two more operators, and get a nail tech to do manicures and pedicures. These new people would pay me enough rent for their stations to pay all the bills, rent included. Once I got the nail station, there would be even more revenue coming in. I even planned to buy a tanning bed, and sell hair products too.

Art liked my drive. He asked me a lot of questions and I tried to answer them professionally. When we came back, he and Dolores went in the back room and closed the door, which was frustrating because I couldn't hear what they were saying. But I needed to pay attention to my haircutting anyway. Remember, I was still new to this and needed to establish a rapport with each customer and make them feel special while they were in my chair. I loved that part of the job. But the whole time I was thinking about the conversation going on in that back room. I had a great feeling – excitement and nervousness rolled into one.

When I was free, I sat with Art in the back and Dolores was out front. We went over the total cost to run the place. Dolores told him how much she'd been earning and I gave him my measly income figures thus far.

I was scared when he said, "You aren't making enough to pay the bills here, pay a loan payment and take home enough money to support yourself and the kids. You would have to rent the extra chairs out to survive. On paper it's doable, but what if you don't find anyone? What if things don't go your way?"

I assured him that I'd work my plan. I'd work as many hours as I had to work to repay him. I showed him again and said I just knew it would work. I would buy the nail station and a tanning bed as soon as I got enough money.

"Peggy, there isn't enough meat on the bone for you to pay me back. Even if I charged a tiny bit of interest, you will be struggling. Your apartment rent is higher than you can afford. You could make it for a while because you saved the money. That money will run out and then what are you going to do then?"

My heart sank. I felt like it was my only chance in the world. It was certainly my biggest hope and dream so far. I just couldn't take no for an answer. I knew I could make it work.

"I will make more money as time goes by," I told him. "I know I will pick up some of her clients because Dolores isn't working anymore. I love it here. What am I going to do if I lose the clientele I have been building up? What if the person who buys it doesn't want me here and takes my customers? I don't want to find a new place to work, things are going great here. I learned in school that it's hard to build a business if you move around. You lose people every time you change salons." Then I added, "How short am I? And what can I do to make it work?"

He smiled and said, "You aren't short at all. I already paid her for the salon. We agreed on thirty-five hundred. I will pay one year's rent, and one year of business insurance. I will buy you the nail station and all you need to make this your own. I'm also going to give you a thousand dollars to keep in the business account and twenty-thousand for a down payment on a house. Shop well and your mortgage will be less than your rent and payment that will not go up unless taxes go up. This will give you a good start on your life. You will be able to manage it if you are wise with your money. You have already shown me you are."

I sat there, speechless and completely overwhelmed. Certainly this was too good to be true... only it wasn't. He was being so kind to me even after I rejected his romantic advances. Unbelievable! How could this have happened to me?

God, I thank You for the miracle. Rags to riches with no strings attached!

After that, everything started happening really fast. I put help wanted signs in the front and back windows the first day I took ownership. And on day two, I hired Mary and Annette, a hairdresser and a barber. They would both stay the whole time I owned the salon. I also hired another hairdresser and a nail tech. I had to manage it, but they paid me enough in chair leases to pay all the expenses and I made money from selling products and my own clientele. Life was great. I still couldn't believe the blessing I'd been given, a bright new start in life.

I called a realtor named Pam, who I had met through my best friend Cris. She turned out to be a true Godsend; not only did she teach me about loans and real estate, we connected in a very personal way. I had lost my husband and my life and was working toward rebuilding something better for myself. She had recently lost a son and was actively grieving. The first time we went out looking at houses we ended up sitting in her car, parked in the driveway of a vacant house, sharing our stories, our hearts, our joys, and our sorrows. We sat there together for over an hour, talking and crying and laughing as the day turned to dusk. I loved her from then on and we are still friends today.

Pam was relatively new to real estate those thirty years ago, but went on to be in the top five percent of realtors in the country, year after year! Magnificent, blessed, and beautiful all in one package. The real deal. Once again, thank you, God!

I told her I had twenty thousand for a down payment and bad credit. Oh yes, I had bad credit because of my connection to Mark. I had paid what we agreed on; he'd paid nothing. I took my car back to the dealer when we split. He drove his until they repossessed it. In addition, I had a brand-new job and little income. That's when Pam told me about "blind assumptions" – when you take a house sight unseen and "as is." It was one of the only ways, she said, that I would get approved.

To add more pressure, I needed to find it fast because Jon was still in Romania and expecting us to buy a house together as soon as he got back. Oh yeah, remember him? Yikes! Was he ever in for a big shock? I had changed my life so much.

Pam found me a house and I got the financing, but as she had said it was through a blind assumption, and a real mess. I didn't care, though. It was mine and the mortgage payment was less than rent. What I lacked in money I more than made up for in energy. My friends and family came over and helped me clean and paint and fix up the yard. We made it a home. Not an attic or a room in someone else's apartment, or the two-bedroom apartment we were moving from. The kids didn't have to share a room anymore. We had a big yard and a nice neighborhood. I had a fresh start. Amazing!

I don't know why I was given such a great blessing, but I accepted it. I also had no way of knowing that this was my parting gift from Art, that he would soon be moving on. Unfortunately, he moved on to a young gold-digger named Diane who worked as a cashier at Safeway and told him anything he wanted to hear. He bought her a brand-new car, a tile roof, paid for vacations for her and her husband, and all kinds of other things that I'd refused to let him buy me. She was using him and he knew it, but he didn't mind. She flirted with him and hugged him and kissed him. Told him she would marry him that day if she weren't already married. She was everything he needed her to be. The more he saw her, the less he called me.

It was sad watching her take so much, and I felt guilty that I hadn't spent more time with him – maybe then he wouldn't be getting played by a money-hungry witch. But something else was bothering me as well. Why wasn't I happy that he didn't call me all the time? Why didn't I feel relief that he didn't need me constantly? I guess I was used to having that special place in his life. Sometimes I thought I should have gotten a house with him; it would have made things easier for the both of us, but he had simply wanted more than I could give.

Finally, after three years his kids realized what was happening and went to court and got control of the money. I have no way of knowing how much she spent before that happened, because we had drifted apart. Debbie also had Mondays off and he chose her companionship over mine. That hurt because I really did enjoy talking to him and hearing all of his old stories of long ago. He had changed my life forever.

Jon did come back and there was hell to pay. He was a completely different man from the one I had known. His brown hair had turned grey in just a few months! I am not sure what had happened to him in Romania, but I was done with him. I told him I was sorry but I wouldn't be marrying him. I gave him back his ring.

After that I decided not to date for a while. I couldn't trust myself, and I had no intention of having a bunch of guys around my kids. My life was expanding and it was great meeting people and doing new things, but I was good with being single and getting better every day. I was actually happy.

That year, I had been blessed beyond measure. It completely changed my life. And remember, this all transpired because I was kind to a lonely old man who came in for a haircut. He was more than fifty years older than me and had a very different kind of life, yet we found friendship. I only had time to share, nothing else. But I gave it willingly for no reason and I was repaid exponentially. Be kind to others. *Always.*

Moving On

Once I got my wings, there was no stopping me. The chairs at the salon were full and bringing in enough to pay all my bills. Then I went to real estate school, figuring I could make big chunks of money and still enjoy daily income from cutting hair. Just as important, I was meeting so many people. Hard to imagine that in just a few years I had gone from babysitting every day to living in this new and exciting world. It was more than great. It was utterly amazing!

At twenty-nine, I was busy with my new house, my kids, friends and family, and the career I had always dreamed of. When I wasn't working at the salon or selling real estate, I was having BBQs and going to the river in the summer. But Jon kept calling me and he was so unhappy. I remember him coming over on Halloween; I answered the doorbell expecting trick-or-treaters. The kids were out with friends and I was home alone and when I saw him there, I was scared. I didn't know why; I hadn't been afraid of him before that. I let him in and we sat down for a few minutes at the table. He just wanted to talk and left without incident, and I thought my uneasiness had been for nothing, thank God.

But then I started seeing him drive by my salon. Someone was calling my house and hanging up when I answered. Several times I had a feeling somebody was looking in my windows at night, and though I never saw anyone I knew it was real, and I knew it was Jon.

I called the police. "I am so sorry," I told them, "but I am scared. I think there is someone lurking around here. I know someone is watching me."

I think I called three times and sure enough, one time the cops did find footprints in the wet grass by the backdoor and under my bedroom window. They told me to lock the gate and make sure I kept everything locked up, which I did.

My thirtieth birthday came; it was a work night and the kids were at my parents. I was celebrating with a few friends – not so much my birthday, but the third anniversary of Mark leaving me. I had already met my goal: my life was better than his, and far better than it had been when we were together! Yippie!

I came in about nine p.m. – not too late because I had to work in the morning – and for some reason put my keys on the table next to the front door. I also kicked off my shoes there. This was not my habit; it was my guardian angel. I felt a little uneasy, but not too bad. I wasn't looking behind the shower curtain, behind doors, or just leaving the house, like I had done several times before. I did check the back door; it was locked. I felt safe. But when I went into my room, there was Jon, lying crossways on my bed. He looked and smelled like he'd been drinking.

"How did you get in here?" I shouted. "Get out!"

"Where have you been? Who were you with on Valentine's Day?"

"None of your business! Get out!"

Now he was shouting too. "Where were you?"

"I'm calling the police!"

I started walking away to go to the phone, but as I reached the doorway he grabbed me by the hair with such force that I was pulled back into the room. He got me down on the bed. Before I knew what was happening, I was being choked! He was standing on the floor, leaning over me with all his might. His full strength was around my neck, so tight I couldn't scream. I could not push him off me. My hands were not able to push his forearms away; I couldn't pry his fingers that were firmly planted around my neck.

Oh God! Please don't let him kill me, I prayed.

I'm not sure where I got the strength or the gumption, but somehow I got my knees up to my chest, in between our bodies, and was able to kick him off me. He went back a few feet and hit the dresser – hard. The tv that was on top of it came crashing down; hopefully, it landed on him. I didn't turn back to see.

I ran for my life to the front door where my keys and shoes were waiting. I grabbed them on the way out. As I got in my car and locked the doors, I saw him in the doorway. I think he may have been saying, "I'll leave" I'm not sure. I honestly didn't care what he said. I drove away and called the police from a pay phone. I was so shaken, so afraid he'd come driving up. My voice was shaking and raspy, my throat hurt so bad as I gave them my address. Then I drove to my parents' house. My mom was out at bingo. My dad and my two kids asleep inside.

I was emotionally and physically overwrought. My head hurt where he'd pulled my hair to jerk me back into the room. My neck felt bruised, my throat was so sore I could barely swallow. I was also embarrassed to have gotten involved with that maniac. Mostly, I felt lucky to be alive. What if he'd killed me? What about my kids? They had already lost their father. I sat outside my parents' apartment and cried my heart out. Happy Stinking Thirtieth Birthday. Finally, I pulled myself together and went inside.

I went in the room with my kids and got into bed with Melissa. I left my turtleneck sweater on so they wouldn't see the hand marks that were already on my neck. I heard Mom come in, but I wasn't ready to talk about it so I stayed in the room and tried to get to sleep. I wondered when I'd get my voice back. More importantly, what was I going to do to stop this from happening again? I was so scared.

I had barely Dozed off when I was startled by a knock at the door. It was the police; Jon had told them that we were at my house for my birthday and had a few drinks. I got mad, he said, and freaked out and injured him when I kicked him in the ribs. He was now at the hospital.

I told my story with my sore, raspy voice: "Officer, I have not been drinking. He and I broke up months ago. I have called the police to that address several times lately, because I know he's been stalking me. I was out with friends until thirty minutes before *I called 911* tonight. I am the one who fled my own home and called you. I wasn't celebrating anything with him. I hadn't spoken to him at all in months. He was in my bedroom, uninvited, when I got home. I don't even know how he got in! The doors were locked. Yes, I did kick him as hard as I could. I was scared. He was trying to kill me!"

I then pulled down the turtleneck to show them what he had done. You could tell by the look on their faces, it was bad. You could hear it in my voice too. They asked me if I wanted to press charges and I told them I didn't know yet. I was too shaken up to think. I figured they wouldn't keep him in jail for doing this to me. What would he do when he got out? I'd just probably get a restraining order.

My dad was horrified. Why hadn't I told him? I had figured, what good would it do? Mom and Dad stayed up and we talked for a while. I would probably rent out the house and get an apartment there, I was too scared to go back. By then it was after midnight and I'd had a long day. I had just fallen asleep again when there was another knock at the door. What the heck? This time, I stood in the hall while my dad answered. It was Jon, asking if I was there.

Dad gave him two seconds to leave before he called the police.

"I don't know what happened," Jon said. "I woke up in the hospital. The police said she hurt me. I have cracked ribs."

That was it. "Get away from here," Dad snarled, "and stay away from her. If you come near her again, she will press charges. You tried to kill her, you little son of a bitch. Now get the hell out of here or you will find yourself in jail! Do you get me? Go!"

He left and I never saw Jon again. He'd always been afraid of getting arrested. He was here legally but believed that if he got arrested he would be deported. He wanted his citizenship and didn't want to take that chance, I guess. Thank God, he left me alone. Still, I did move out of the house; I no longer felt safe there. I rented it out and we got an apartment right by my parents.

Fast forward a few years, and a funny end to that story.

I was at work and I got a call from Jon. I told him I didn't want to talk to him. He said, "Please my dear, take the hex off me."

"What are you talking about? That's ridiculous, what hex?"

"Please, I am begging you. I know you are close to God. I know you cursed me for what I did. Please ask Him to remove the curse. My life has been so bad since we broke up."

"Jon, I'm hanging up, this is crazy. I am at work. I have customers here."

"Can I come over there? Can I call you tonight? Please!" He was begging.

"No, stay away from me, and don't ever call me again and I will remove the curse."

I couldn't help but smirk.

The phone was at the reception desk and the reception desk was in earshot of several people. At the salon we had a light, fun, family atmosphere, but still... I stood there for all to hear and said, "Okay, Jon, the curse is removed. You can go and live a good life. From this day on, I wish you peace and happiness."

"Thank you, Peggy."

"Goodbye, Jon."

You can believe I am laughing out loud as I write this. It was so stinking funny!

After Jon, I purposely spent a few years alone. It was fine, I had my best girlfriends to get me through the hard patches and lots of family around all the time. I realized I actually liked the independence and the freedom that came with being single. I also still didn't feel I could be trusted to pick my men. I was busy working and had my kids. It was enough. But then a few years later I met Dean.

Chapter Six

TRYING AGAIN

Have you ever just been tired? I don't mean tired like you need to get some sleep. I'm not referring to being tired of someone or something like a car or a neighbor you don't like. Tired of getting short-changed at the store or disrespected by a coworker. Tired of the same rerun playing on tv or the same rerunning thoughts in your head. I'm talking about tired of *everything*! My mom called it Plain Damn Tired.

After three years of being a single mother of two, I got tired. I felt like I was running a race that had no finish line. No rest area. Nothing to look forward to. I had been pulling myself up life's ladder, but it was exhausting. Things were getting better in my life, emotionally and financially, but they were still not too great. As usual, I needed more and I was willing to work for it, if only I knew how to get it faster. If only I knew what it was that I wanted. I was exhausted, and I didn't know how long I could keep it up. Yes, I was Plain Damn Tired.

That's when I met Dean.

Dean was fun, quick-witted, and he was always laughing. Everyone liked him. He was the kind of person that you just knew had a great heart. You could see it in his eyes. He was always joking around, and though his jokes were corny they were funny too. He had a good job and was generous.

I had met him the year before at a restaurant that served brunch and played the San Francisco 49ers games – my favorite team and, it turned out, Dean's as well. We had chatted a bit that first time but didn't connect. But the next season I saw him there again and we hit it off. It didn't hurt that he was a friend of a friend, which made him easier to trust.

He invited me to Seattle to watch a Seahawks game – my first live NFL game ever. I found him funny, smart, and super-easy to talk to. He loved kids and had none of his own. No ex-wife either, which was a plus. It was hard to meet a guy with no kids and no ex, especially now that I was in my thirties. After a while I introduced him to my kids and they liked him right away.

Tyler, who was about six at the time, asked him in their first conversation, "Are you gonna marry my mom? I need a dad. My dad lives in California. My mom works a lot, and we don't have enough money. Do you have a lot of money?"

Dean didn't run. He sat there with my boy and told him it was too soon to tell what would happen. He let him know we are still getting to know each other. He said moms have to be really careful because they have kids to take care of, and kids are very important. They can't let just anybody into their family. Then he let him know that he thought my kids had a great mom; and the reason he knew that was because Tyler was a great kid. I think that was the moment I decided I would allow myself to love Dean.

Later on, when I walked him to his car, he sang me a song to the tune of Barney:

"I love you; you love me. Ty wants us to be a family..."

I don't remember the rest but I think there was more. He would sing it often.

We had fun together, but I did work a lot. I owned my hair salon and worked there to pay the bills every month. And since I was also a realtor, I had to show houses and meet with clients in the evenings and on weekends when they were off work. I also had bought a fixer-upper, which I loved. It was a three-family house, built in 1908. Full of charm, with thick woodwork, built-in cabinets, and a long stairway with a rail the kids could slide down. It had a porch that wrapped around two sides. The front door was the original, with detailed scrolling and side lights. This old house was beautiful, but nobody could see in it what I saw.

To be honest, you had to use your imagination to see the beauty. It had old, hideous carpet, and unfortunately it wasn't only on the floor. Seriously, there were twelve-by-twelve carpet squares nailed to at least five or six walls! On the main floor, the cupboards were all missing or broken. There were so many rotten boards on the porch it was dangerous to walk on. Oh, and the roof! There were many shingles missing, but fortunately they were only missing on one side. I put boards on the rafters in the attic so I could walk up there. Then I put coffee cans and buckets and towels and tarps down. And well, we did pretty good, depending on the amount of rainfall – which in Oregon is a lot.

Everything was great at first, but then October came, and it was plenty rainy until July. Me and the kids would have to go up there and work our system to empty the buckets regularly or they would definitely leak into the house through the ceiling. Sometimes it would pour for hours and I'd have to do it twice in a day because the little buckets at the edge would fill up so fast. It was a simple and painless process, just a pain in the butt that you had to do it at all. I couldn't forget or I'd be really sorry. I'd go to the attic and empty the little buckets into a little bigger one with a handle. I had a couple that were the kids' sand pails, which worked perfect and didn't get too heavy. Then I'd pass that one down to Tyler, who stood on a ladder with his head in the attic so he could see. He would hand it to my daughter or one of my friends or family members, if they were there. It was much easier and faster with three people so it came in handy that I had a lot of friends. I had help.

There were three apartments and none of them were in good shape. When I bought the house, I inherited the tenants. There was a young couple in the basement paying two hundred and fifty a month, and a girl upstairs paying three hundred. I wanted to get the main floor unit ready so I could let her live there. This would allow me to take care of the buckets of rainwater without disturbing her. I felt awful having to access her apartment every time it rained, but I hadn't known of the problem until shortly after I bought the house.

Maybe I was naïve or just too inexperienced. I know I did not understand how essential a good roof is; I just didn't know how badly it needed it and how quickly I would need to come up with the money to get it redone. The prior owner did tell me the roof was in bad shape and needed to be replaced. He even lowered the price by five thousand dollars to compensate. He was fair, I just didn't have the other five thousand in the first place. Now I knew I had to get a roof ASAP. I just had to sell a house or two. But what I really had to do was fix the third apartment so I could rent that too. This would give me enough to make the house payment without taking any money out of my pocket, plus a bit extra to work on renovations. I was also still paying rent at the apartment we were living in. No one knew what bad shape I was in, because I was too embarrassed to tell them. I don't think anyone agreed with my decision to buy it in the first place. My dad was against it right from the start.

He told me, "Sweetie, I have faith in you, but I think you may be biting off more than you can chew this time."

To make things worse, the house had no insurance on it because I had cancelled the expensive policy the prior owner had and went to Allstate. When they inspected the house, they said no way they could insure it. Too many hazards, including branches touching the roof and siding, cracked and broken windows, missing shingles, and those rotten boards on the porch.

They'd have found lots more, but they only inspected the outside.

I quickly fixed everything but the roof but they still wouldn't accept the risk. I called the other company back but they too looked at the roof and failed the inspection. Now I had no insurance, and I was in breach of contract; the previous owner could take the house back if he knew it. Worse than that, what if it burned down and I lost everything? What if someone got hurt and I had no insurance? During those months I remember just lying in bed at night with my eyes wide open, looking up at the ceiling, worrying and praying. Praying and worrying. It was awful. I was almost worried sick – literally! I was doing the best I could to pay all my bills, take care of the salon and the kids, and spending everything else on fixing up that third apartment.

I didn't know anyone who had money to help me. Even if I did, I wasn't able to make any kind of payment plan fit into the already tight budget. I never knew how much I was going to make from day to day or month to month. My daughter was in middle school and needed things. I wanted her to have the essentials and more. I owed her that, I promised myself that my kids would have what they needed – nice clothes and shoes and coats and sports and movies and sleepovers. I wanted them to just be normal kids in a decent neighborhood, which they were, and I was willing to do anything I could to keep it that way.

So, back to Dean.

I have to admit that early on I realized that he may not be the best match for me. I loved working on houses and yards. He had never even picked up a hammer or a shovel, nor was he interested in doing so. If he called and I was busy at the house he never offered to help. He just made a plan for when I had time to go out, which wasn't more than once a week. I had lots on my plate and would have loved the help. I got lonely over there at night after work. He didn't try to talk me out of working, which I appreciated, but I wanted a rugged guy who worked with his hands. Back then, I still thought that most, if not all, men knew how to fix things around the house, so Dean shocked me.

One day I was taking down kitchen cabinets with Tyler when Dean called to see if I wanted to meet for dinner.

"No, I can't. We need to get these cabinets down before we can leave. I am planning on painting this kitchen tomorrow and I need it to be empty."

Now, my perfect guy would have said, "Oh, I'll come over and help you. It will go faster and then we can grab something to eat."

Not Dean. He said something like, "Well maybe you can get done earlier tomorrow and we can see each other then."

He told me later that when I said "we" all those times he thought I had a guy over there. He wasn't sure he wanted to know who it was, so he didn't ask. Yes, I had a lot of friends and many were male. And many of them did help me a lot! For that I am eternally grateful.

There was no shortage of men, both friends and admirers – several of whom I met at my salon. I got asked out a lot. Most guys I met tried to get me to work less. I couldn't. How would the job get done if I didn't do it? I decided if they weren't on the same page they weren't for me. Truth be told, there was no time for a relationship unless working on the house could be a date. I worked Tuesday through Saturday at the salon. I worked at real estate after work and weekends and on the house most evenings. Other than that, I was home with the kids. On Sundays we went to church and then hung out with the family. Back then most of my siblings went to our parents' house every Sunday. I loved it, and I made it a priority. I needed this family time to refresh myself. Even when I had an open house to meet with potential buyers, I always got done as quickly as possible.

I am a list-maker. A goal-setter. A worker. I like that about me. As far back as I can remember, I've started each day with a written plan, a road map so I know where I'm going. I'd sit down in the morning, do a crossword puzzle, and think about the day, about the week ahead. What do I need to do? How long will it take? How much will it cost? What do I need to get it done? Time. Money, help? Then I write my list and LOVE to check things off the list. If I don't get it done that day, it goes to the top of the next day. It helps me stick to the plan, and not procrastinate.

At that time, I definitely needed a plan, as I was juggling my kids, my business, my home, and my investment in my future. I wanted a guy who wanted to help me and I never seemed to meet that guy. So by this time I was tired. Plain Damn Tired.

Dean was generous. I didn't like to ask for things, but I mentioned needing to stay at the salon more hours to earn quick money for supplies for the house. He got me a Home Depot gift card. So thoughtful. What a perfect gift for me. Another time when I asked if he'd help me paint on a weekend he said, "I'll go to work, make extra money and you can pay a painter." I didn't take him up on that, but I really appreciated the offer. The house was my project and responsibility. But it did help me understand him better. He wasn't a painter.

My dad would have loved to help but he worked full-time and still had no money, ever. My parents did help with the kids all the time – dropping them off, picking them up and babysitting for me. I couldn't have done it without them. And when they thought I wasn't spending enough time with the kids, they let me know that too. They kept me in check because I probably would have slept in a sleeping bag in that run-down house if it saved me gas money and gave me more time to work.

Dean was the opposite. He was a procrastinator. He didn't make a lot of goals. Mostly, he liked to go to work and watch tv, though on the weekends he loved going out to his uncle's farm and hanging out with his family. It was only twenty-five miles away from the city, but a completely different world – very relaxing and peaceful. I loved that about him too.

He had had an accident a few years prior to us getting together. His body hurt sometimes, but he never complained. He had a rod in his hip, which got kind of stiff in the cold. It was a bad accident that broke bones, ruptured his spleen, and lacerated his liver. He had quit drinking after that accident. He had been drinking that night and though he said he wasn't drunk he shouldn't have gotten behind the wheel either. Well, this was great news for me. I had been married to an alcoholic already and it stunk. I had sworn not to date drinkers, so at least I didn't have to worry about that.

I figured he didn't make physical goals due to his body aches, but he was great at his job and made good money. I thought it was amazing that he could fix a phone system a thousand miles away from a laptop in my living room. This was the early nineties, and I had never heard of anything like it. He was ahead of his time, and got calls from headhunters offering him jobs all over the country. He was "The Duke of Dial Tone" to friends and colleagues. He did have to go to school for new systems and computers, sometimes out of town, to keep up on new certifications.

I could appreciate his work ethic, and I used to tell him we should go into business together. He could install and repair the phone systems; I'd do everything else. We could have been successful at it, I know. But Dean didn't have the same drive as I had. He had no interest in owning a company. It was disappointing to me, but like I said he had other attributes. I came to understand what his friends had all known: he was brilliant. I didn't appreciate brilliant; I was looking for strong and hardworking. I wanted someone who could see what needed to be done and wanted to do it. That just wasn't him. I used to love to go for walks and play cards with friends. Not for him either. But, as mentioned, we did both like football, and he loved the few friends we had in common. We liked each other's families as well. His Uncle Bill had found a five-acre plot that was a great deal and encouraged Dean to buy it. Now, that was my cup of tea. Dean sold his monster truck for the down payment. The goal was to build a house someday. There was a plan I could respect.

I had met a lot of men in the five years I'd been single, and Dean seemed to hit the mark on most of the things I wanted. Number one, he loved me and the kids. I may not have had that crazy-in-love, "can't eat, can't sleep" feeling about him, but I did love him too. When Dean asked me to marry him, I happily said yes.

Dean was a great addition to our little family. My kids were crazy about him, and he added a lighthearted spin to my stressful life. I had always been way too serious and he made me laugh. It was nice to relax a bit. It was nice to have a partner, especially one with a good job and good medical benefits. He didn't mind if I worked a lot, plus, he agreed that I was better with money than he was and turned his paychecks over to me to do the budget and pay the bills.

They say that mad passion is overrated anyway. How long would the fireworks really last? I hate to admit I knowingly married a man who may not have been perfect, but who is? I really did love him, and did I mention I was Plain Damn Tired?

Our wedding was easy to plan. Dean hadn't been married before and didn't care if we had a big wedding, small wedding, at home or church, or if we eloped. We settled on a simple but fun affair. Of course, there is more to the story; this was not my "happily ever after" – dammit!

His parents came up from Arizona for the wedding and I was happy to have them. They stayed at my house and I set up a room for them in the dining room. I barely knew them; I had met them once on a short visit to Arizona and had several phone conversations with Marilyn, his mother. She was a very large women and could not make it up the stairs where the bedrooms were. We made do. I was perfectly comfortable and believe they were too. The night before the wedding we had a rehearsal and went out for dinner. At the end of the evening me and the kids went home with Dean's parents. Dean still had an apartment and went home. We would see each other at the wedding the next day. We were both excited and so were the kids, our friends and our families. The kids were up in their rooms already in bed and I was sitting with the parents in the living room, getting ready to say our goodnights.

Then the phone rang.

Remember Jody? Well, it was him on the other end of the phone. He just happened to call, out of the blue, the night before my wedding!

As he said hello, I could hear his impish grin in his voice. I could picture his face, his smile. I hadn't seen him in nearly half my life – literally. I was sixteen years old then and that had been fifteen years ago. Aside from the call when I first married Mark, he had reached out a couple of times, but that was several years ago. None of that mattered. Just hearing his voice, I smiled big and broad. I was warmed up inside. It was crazy, the pull on my heart he still had.

I was also, once again, talking on a phone that was not cordless, so there I sat in my living room with my soon to be in-laws, talking to the love of my life. I could not excuse myself; I was stuck to the wall. His parents didn't have the courtesy to give me privacy; they just sat, side by side, about three feet away from me. They didn't even pretend not to eavesdrop! How rude.

"Do you know who this is?"

"Of course I do," I said with a smile. "How are you? What are you up to?"

"I'm truck driving now and I was just thinking about you. I wanted to tell you I've never forgotten you. I still want to see you again. "

When I left New York, we had "our song" – James Taylor's Fire and Rain, so Jody's words about seeing me again were especially significant. It was our secret, only ours.

"Well, where are you?" I asked.

"I'll be heading to the West Coast for several trips with this company I work for. I was hoping we could make a plan to meet. "

"I'm so sorry, I can't do that, I am getting married tomorrow."

I was so overwhelmed with emotion. Why hadn't he called six months ago? Why now?

"Do you love him?" Jody asked.

"Yes. I do."

What else could I say? Truth is, I did love Dean. He was a great man. Yet I had tears in my eyes. Holy crap, what was happening? I just knew I wasn't hiding my feelings; I was wearing my emotions all over my face. I needed to pull myself together. I wished I could talk to Jody freely. I wished I could ask for his number without them hearing me. I wish he'd have called after they went to bed.

Jody just said, "Wow, bad timing. I wish you luck. I hope you're happy."

"Okay, nice to talk to you again. Good bye," I said.

What I didn't say was, *Call me in an hour. I could be happier. I still love you. I'm not crazy in love like I should be the night before my wedding. When will you be here? Where can we meet? I always thought I'd see you again.*

I could barely contain myself. I hung up the phone, said goodnight to the parents as quick as I could and went up in my room and cried. What was I doing? Jody had moved on. I had moved on. I didn't even ask if he was still married. Yes, he had gotten married – I had learned that when we spoke years earlier. He was probably lonely, I thought, and just wanted to talk as a friend. I was not going to throw away my life with Dean for a teenager's first love.

Get it together, Peggy. Everything is going to work out just fine.

I could hear his parents talking downstairs and wondered if I should go back down and confront this head-on. After all, I was marrying their son the next day. Dean knew all about Jody. I was honest. I had told him about my few love affairs during our courting period. He knew the whole story: how it was my first love, how I was pulled away. How we were supposed to get married when I turned eighteen. How we'd talked over the years but were never single at the same time. Dean already knew, so why was I so worried about the parents? And why the hell did they just sit there listening anyway? It was clearly a private conversation. As it turned out I didn't have to decide what to do. About twenty minutes after I went to bed, Dean came over. I could hear him talking to his parent. I was getting ready to go down and see why he was there when he came up to my room.

"Lovey, are you okay?' he asked.

"Yeah, I'm fine. Why are you back here?"

"I can see you are crying. My mom called and said you were clearly upset. She is concerned and wondering what's going on."

She was not concerned. She was pissed. We both knew it.

I grabbed my bathrobe and went downstairs so we could talk it out. She needed to know I was an honest person; I like to get to the bottom of things and the sooner the better. When I got down there, I made light of the call. Old boyfriend, overwhelmed because of the wedding, tired, stressed out... and Marilyn would have none of it.

"The way you looked when that man called you, the way you lit up, looks just like love to me. And that is not the way you look at my son. A mother wants that for her son. Who was that? It is obvious you love him."

I told them the truth. Yes, he was my first love, but I hadn't talked to him in years and hadn't seen him since I was sixteen. This was not anything I was going to act on. I was happy with her son.

Dean came back upstairs with me. We talked about the conversation Jody and I had had. Of course he wanted to know what was said and why he happened to call that day. He asked if I wished I could see him or get back with him. Naturally he wanted to know if he was divorced now and if Jody and I made plans. "No, no, and no," I assured him. "I didn't even ask. I love you. I want to marry you. I have no way to contact him and no plan to see him. I didn't even ask for his phone number."

Dean knew he could trust me. He went back down and talked to his parents a while. I have no idea what they were saying. I didn't really care. It seemed like they were purposely talking quietly, not sure why. I went to sleep emotionally drained. I had a big day to look forward to tomorrow and lots to do.

The next day Marilyn was cold, but who could blame her? That woman saw right through me and called me out on it. She thought her son should know about this person on the other end of the phone. Thank heavens I'd been honest with Dean, so even though the bomb dropped it was quickly defused.

We got married at three in the afternoon in a hall where we had the ceremony and reception. There were about a hundred people there. My dad, my rock, was walking me down the aisle. Everything was set. We were in the back and the music started.

Suddenly I turned to him and said, "Dad, I don't want to get married." I pulled back gently on his arm that was hooked to mine.

"What? Why?"

"Jody called me last night. My heart still loves him. I don't think you should get married to someone when you wonder if you should be with someone else."

"Why did he call? What did he say to you to make you change your mind?"

"Nothing," I swore. "Dad, he didn't have to say anything. I don't even know if he is single right now. It was a one-minute conversation with Marilyn and Harold sitting there listening. It doesn't matter what he says, don't you see? I just feel like I still love him, it never goes away."

"Why are you doing this? Dean is a great guy. He loves you and the kids; he can take care of you. Life will be much easier for you. You don't have to do it alone anymore. You are marrying him," he insisted as he tugged me down the aisle by our joined elbows. "Don't be silly Sweetie, you can't just throw this away. I can't let you leave him at the altar."

"Dad, please, we can have the party. I'll talk to Dean. He already knows about Jody. I'll just tell him I'm not sure. Please, Dad. Let me go back and you go up and tell everyone the wedding is off. We'll still have the party."

All of this dialogue happened while we were walking down the aisle. But once I was there, hand in hand with Dean, kids by my side, I wondered, *What do I do? Stop the wedding while I stand here in front of all our family and friends? No,* I decided, *Dad's right. I'm tired of this. I am tired of being alone. Dean is a great guy; I really do love him. Jody is a fairy tale prince charming. Not a reality. I don't even know him anymore. I haven't talked to him more than thirty minutes total in the past fifteen years. I have a responsibility to my kids. I want them to have a good life. Dean has a good job and loves us.*

The ceremony was officiated by a good friend of mine, Denny Strong, who I had met at real estate school. He was a great Christian man and an ordained minister. So nice to have a friend like that.

I'm not sure I heard a word Denny said, but I remember saying, "I do."

The party had been planned to the last detail. My sisters and I made the food, friends decorated, and my brothers, who are very talented musicians, were the band. Dean and I were going to leave the party around ten to go to a nice hotel for the night and then spend Sunday with our families and best friends. We also needed to see off our out-of-town guests. Then Monday we'd leave for a week-long honeymoon. This was my new life, and it would be a good one.

The party was great, with everyone laughing and singing and dancing. They loved the band and the food and the bride and groom. Unfortunately, without telling me Dean decided to drink. I was very disappointed. I was already wondering if I made the right decision.

The next day we went back to the house and all the festivities. We had a ton of food left over and my sisters were there preparing the feast. Good thing too, because after laughing, talking and dancing all night, we were starving. It was also nice for Dean's parents to get to know my family. Lots of lively conversation and fun. The day went by quickly and we said our goodbyes to everyone and took the parents to the airport. I was tired after the long weekend and glad I had already packed for our trip the next morning.

I thought it was really telling that Dean's groomsmen didn't come over for the post-celebration at the house. I didn't miss them, there were plenty of people there to make a party, but why weren't they there? They knew the party was happening but for some reason it wasn't important to be there. I assumed they were either hungover or watching football, but either way we were not the priority. We had fun, but this tugged at the back of my mind.

I was also still upset that Dean drank – and quite a bit – at the reception. I couldn't be married to another drinker. Oh, God, please not again. It was just so sad to me. He said he was sorry, but the damage had already been done. Maybe I should have called off the wedding. I wasn't sure what I had gotten myself into. I thought I was signing up for love, honor, and cherish, but I certainly didn't feel any of that. In fact, I was wondering if I had been wrong to listen to my dad and go through with the wedding. I had kept my promise to marry Dean and make the most of it, but I was not expecting it to start off like this. My new future, once so promising, now scared the crap out of me. This isn't what I want, not at all.

I called Denny and invited him to come over to the day-after party. I desperately needed to talk to him. He said he had plans with his kids after church and would stop by after that if he could, but that didn't happen.

Early the next morning, while Dean was in the shower and we were getting ready to leave for the week, I called him again.

"Denny, I made a huge mistake. Don't turn in my marriage certificate. I am not sure I want to be married."

"Are you okay, Peggy? What happened?"

I let him know I only had a minute, then gave him the day's story in brief. I let him know that was why I begged him to come over the day before. Nobody else knew anything about how I was feeling. Denny had met with us for counseling several times prior to the wedding. He knew this was not what I signed up for.

"Peggy, I'm sorry, I had no idea. I dropped that off at the post office when I left the ceremony Saturday afternoon. We can get together and talk about it when you guys get back."

That was not what I wanted to hear. In my life I go by the idea that there are no accidents and everything happens for a reason. That would include this crazy turn of events. I told myself, *God must have wanted this. I am not going to go crazy trying to change what is. I am officially and legally married. I will do the best I can to be a good wife. I will trust Dean that he won't be drinking anymore. I believe he will be a great husband and dad to Melissa and Tyler. I will plan on having a fun and loving family with my new husband and my kids.*

Dean and I had made a deal that for the first three months of our marriage I would not take birth-control. If I got pregnant, it was God's plan. If I did not, he agreed to be happy with the two we already had and not ask me again to try to conceive. Now I was reconsidering that deal. I knew I could justify it in my own mind and heart without any guilt. I wouldn't have to feel bad at all if I reneged under the circumstances. I had the right to make sure I knew who I was married to before having another child. I had just spent years taking care of Melissa and Tyler alone, even when I was still with Mark. They were my kids, and except financially while we were married, they had been my sole responsibility. Not to mention that before that I had taken care of my siblings for years. Before meeting Dean I had never planned on having any more kids, not when I finally had a little freedom. I certainly didn't want to start over with a new baby if this marriage was doomed from the start.

In the end I decided to keep my word. I had just gotten married and I didn't want to plan on it failing. That was an awful feeling. Just because he broke a promise by getting drunk at our wedding didn't mean I should pay him back with breaking this promise to have a baby. I would be a woman who keeps her promises. I would love honor and cherish him, "'til death do us part." I would make the most of this marriage with a good attitude of hope and love, and pray he did too.

I didn't know what I was in for...

I still am not a hundred percent certain today, but I think Dean continued drinking often after our wedding day and must have been very good at hiding it. I don't know how quickly his return to full-fledged alcoholism came about. I do know that I didn't know how bad his problem once had been; how much he struggled with it for the year prior to the marriage; and how it would affect our lives in the future. I hadn't seen him drink in the first few months of our marriage and, happily, I did get pregnant right away. Despite my earlier feelings, I found I was excited about having a new baby and even more excited to tell Dean. Oh my gosh, a dream come true for him. He is going to be the happiest man on earth.

On the day I had a positive pregnancy test, I had Melissa and Tyler go to my parents for the night. I made Dean's favorite dinner of rack of lamb and roasted red potatoes and parsley carrots. He told me he'd be home around six or so, and I set a beautiful dinner table with candles and all. But there was no Dean – not at six, six-thirty, or seven. He did get busy, I knew; he worked on companies' phone systems and often couldn't leave until it was up and running. He must be stuck at work, I told myself.

I paged him several times. No call back, no Dean. *Why doesn't he call me back? He knows I'm waiting for him. He has no idea about the news I am about to give him. This is supposed to be a great day, the day we start a new chapter in our lives.* I didn't want to worry, but I couldn't help it. I wanted to be happy, but now I was sad. I wanted to be excited when he walked in the door, but now I was pissed. No matter what was happening, where he was, the surprise was ruined. Surely there's a phone he could find to call on and let me know he was okay. I had been disrespected once again. Finally I decided I had no choice but to put the food away and clean up the table. It wasn't dinner time anymore.

Dean came in around nine o'clock...and he was drunk.

"I'm sorry, Lovey," he said, a silly grin on his face. "I got caught up with an old friend. I was only going to have one drink but I ended up staying out way too long."

"You've been *drinking*?"

"Don't be mad at me. I didn't do it on purpose. I'm sorry, I won't do it again," he lied.

He tried to make light of it. Tried to be funny, wanted me to laugh with him and welcome him home with open arms; Afterall, we were newlyweds. I wanted none of it.

I went to bed without telling him about the beautiful baby that we were going to have. Once again, grief and heartache. What have I done? Why did I do this? I knew he had a drinking problem when I first dated him. I knew it is really hard to quit drinking and not go back. I had promised myself not to get involved with a drinker and I did anyway. Why did I trust him? I wanted to, that's why.

I'd jumped from the frying pan into the fire because I was tired of the rat race, tired of being alone, emotionally and financially. I was looking for an easy way out, or up. He had a great heart; he was a good man. He had a good job and he could take care of us, but not if he was drinking. No matter how good you are at your job, if you are an alcoholic it is very hard to keep it all together. Alcoholics lose jobs every day, so why would Dean be any different?

Truth be told, that night wasn't the first sign of trouble since the wedding; in fact, things had gone downhill fast. We had no sooner gotten married when his paychecks started being garnished. I had sold my salon and paid off his truck. One less payment. After I found out I was pregnant more bills came in. I called payroll at his office, and the woman told me there was one judgment after another – more debts I didn't know he had that were going to be coming out of his checks. I had to refinance my house and make a deal with all the creditors. He was supposed to support me and my kids. This was supposed to be different. Life was supposed to be easier with a partner. Wasn't it?

I was in trouble here, big trouble. I had just dragged my kids into a mess. I promised them a better life and it was already falling apart. How could I have been so stupid to sell the salon and get rid of my source of income? The only thing I could tell myself, which did made me feel okay, was that "God is in control." I had known if I got pregnant in the first few months it was His plan for me. I had prayed that prayer so many times. Now I would have to put my trust in the Lord and believe that He would see me, my kids, and the new baby through this mess.

I had to change my attitude if I was going to keep things going, and I *had* to keep things going. Change the attitude and your life changes immediately. Just because it was not happening the way I expected it to didn't mean it wasn't the right thing for me.

The truth was, I was happy about having a baby. I loved it already and couldn't wait to hold it in my arms, to see what it looked like and to get to know its personality. I had no idea that my little Kimberly would be a great joy to me in my pain, a great companion to me in the future and the most beautiful, sincere person I have ever known. She was my saving grace. Truly a gift from God.

In the meantime, Dean continued to drink. Unbeknownst to me, he had cirrhosis of the liver and *that* was why he had quit drinking before we got together. He had lacerated his liver in the accident he had been in the year before we started dating. His family has a history of unhealthy livers, even with no alcohol consumption. He had never shared any of this. I did not know that the drinking was causing even worse effects than the sadness of a troubled marriage, and the unpredictability that comes with being married to an alcoholic. Poor Dean; It was actually killing the man with every sip and he just could not seem to find a way to stop.

As time went by, he stopped more often than not to have a drink (or drinks) on his way from work, which left us less time together as a family and made it hard to enjoy the moments we did have. The kids were getting older and I tried to hide how sad I was and how unstable our life with him was. They loved him, and he was always good to us. As a matter of fact, the only problem we had with our life was his drinking. We went on family vacations and vacations with just the two of us. We had good friends, we had lots of fun going out of town to NFL games. We had a nice home – my "fixer -upper" was all fixed up, thanks to Dean. He didn't do work himself but he made enough money to pay people to do the things that I could not. Our life could have been wonderful, but unfortunately alcohol won the battle.

Dean died of liver-related causes at the age of thirty-seven. It happened pretty quickly. We found out in August that he needed a liver transplant, but he could not be put on the list until he was sober for a year. He never made it, but passed that February. I was starting over once again, but now with three kids instead of two and my little Kimberly, the apple of her dad's eye, would never know her father's love. She was only three years old. It was so sad. He was so young; and now he was gone forever.

My life had been good with Dean –not overly happy, not ideal or even peaceful, but stable. The kids had a nice life. Dean and I did not fight; when we had a conflict, we figured it out. Our marriage hadn't been the fairy tale I'd hoped for, but I took care of him until the end and when he was gone I missed him. And there was so much to miss: his love, his companionship when he was available, his relationships with the kids, his laughter, and his jokes. Oh, he was funny. I did miss him, the head of the family. Yet sometimes I felt guilty that I didn't feel worse about my loss. Really, I had come to terms with the truth: I lost my husband long before his death. Alcohol stole him from me.

I will always be grateful that Dean and I had made our "prenuptial agreement." No, not a financial agreement – the baby agreement. God always knows what He's doing! Literally, I don't know what I would have done as a thirty-six-year-old widow without Kimberly. Melissa was eighteen, starting her own life. Tyler was thirteen and in eighth grade. We all know how busy kids are when they're in high school. But Kimberly was home with me, my constant companion. God knew I'd be alone so He gave me Kimberly.

Chapter Seven

BUILDING CONFIDENCE

After Dean's death I was pretty lost. I had expected it, but was not prepared at all. I couldn't believe I had to start over again. Then a friend asked me to go halves on a salon with her. I was the one who did hair and could manage the day-to-day and the staff. She would take care of the business side – the books and banking – and would work in the evenings and Saturday. I hired several people right away so there was coverage when we weren't there.

I had just enough life insurance to pay off the house. I am so grateful for that because I had borrowed over seventy thousand dollars just to pay off the bills Dean had. Next, I refinanced it and paid off the loan on the five acres Dean and I bought in the country, then I built a large house there. That took well over a year because I really didn't have much money to spend. I was my own contractor and Dean's uncle Bill helped me with everything. Tyler, Kimberly, and I moved out there, but Melissa had graduated and wouldn't move away from the city. She lived in the basement apartment in our home in town and I rented out the main house.

I worked on the new house and the yard, all day, every day, making it a home for us. But it got pretty lonely out in the woods. I went to town a few days a week to work at the hair salon, but then I'd have to rush back to the kids after school. Lots of driving, lots of gas money. I was out of money for projects, and the winter was setting in. When my renters told me they were leaving Portland, I decided my country adventure was over. It was time to rent out the country house and move back to town.

And Then There Was Fred

I would soon begin an on-again, off-again relationship that lasted for several years. I needed security and I wanted Fred, who was my friend Shelly's boss, to rescue me. He promised me the world. We traveled together and he could afford things for me and the kids that I couldn't. He was fun too, and suddenly my life was so exciting. He swept me off my feet. My perfect prince. He was everything I wanted... or so I thought. Over time, it became clear that he was not the guy on the inside he professed to be outwardly. Oh my gosh, he was really selfish and petty, and our relationship ended up a sad, sad mess. I will just tell you the end in brief.

On Tuesday nights he met two other couples for "a meeting" – which was really a few cocktails and dinner. I didn't always go; I had the kids, plus by that point I was in college (more on that later) and had plenty to do. The last meeting I ever attended was at a Chinese restaurant. I left to go to the bathroom and when I came back I heard him saying to the waitress, "I've been telling you for three weeks, I am not married." Ohhhh, my heart dropped. What a jerk! I said "Damn right, you're not!" I grabbed my purse and left. I was so humiliated.

I went into the lobby and called Shelly. Just as I was asking her through my tears to come and get me, Fred came out and demanded, "Let's go." It was a dark rainy night. I was very upset to say the least. After a few minutes I broke the silence and started bitching at him about everything that had ever happened between us. But this is the last straw. How could he do this to me? How disgusting? Doesn't he realize how humiliating that was? How disrespectful?

He was quickly losing his patience with me. I was not behaving the way I usually did. He didn't like it at all.

"Peggy, enough! Stop talking or get out of the truck!"

"I am NOT getting out of the truck; you will never tell me what to do again. EVER."

He pulled the truck over and started pushing me to the passenger door. "Get out! He shouted.

"I will not! Just bring me to my car, I will be quiet."

It was a dark night, probably only about six or seven but rainy and cold. The road we were on had no sidewalk and no street lights. I wasn't about to get out. I felt safer in the truck than out in the wet, cold, dark night.

He put the truck in park and yelled, "Get out!" again, pushing me toward the door.

"Just go home. I will get my car and leave."

He hopped out of the driver's side and walked across the front of the truck to force me out, I assume.

I didn't give him the chance. As soon as he got to my side, I popped over to the driver's side, locked the doors and sped off. I left him on the road side! In my imagination the rocks and mud were flying in his face as I burned out in the gravel. I was scared as anything; my heart was racing. I don't think I looked back. I went to his house, got my car, and left. I never saw him again. Enough was enough.

What a waste of precious time and energy. Another broken heart. Another relationship I had to work so hard at. And for what? It had led nowhere. I also met a great guy named Rick during that time. I think I could have loved him. I didn't give that one a chance. Perhaps, that could have been worth the effort, but it was bad timing for both of us.

Starting Over Again

I closed that door behind me. What did I want? Where did I see myself in the future? Who was I, really? I had already sold the salon I owned with my friend. My joints were already getting tired of it. My neck hurt from tipping my had down all day and my fingers were beginning to get stiff. I longed for a job with benefits and promotion, and my dream of graduating from college was finally on the horizon. Maybe that would fulfill me.

When Melissa found out she was pregnant my whole world stopped in anticipation of the bundle of joy, Aliza Grace. I had always dreamed of having grandchildren. I'd always felt like an unwanted grandchild, and I vowed that my grandkids would know I adored them. I had also vowed that I would not be a smoking grandma, and now I only had eight months – until Aliza Grace's due date, to honor that promise. But my true self asked, "Why put it off when you could quit now?" I checked the carton I always had on top of the fridge and saw there were three packs left. I decided to quit when that carton ran out, roughly three days. It wasn't set in stone, but a definite possibility.

The very next day the incident with Fred happened. It had been one of those crappy relationships you knew was never going to work. Something happens and you break up, but then for some reason you go back knowing it's leading to the same dead end. Not sure why I kept going back, but I did. I've never been a dater. I just like to go straight for the whole kit and kaboodle.

I know, it's a crazy thing, I'll meet a guy and think he's great, then the pheromones wear off. I open my eyes and see they are not the right guy for me, sometimes I stay and try anyways. I stay way too long, in hopes they will change. I finally get it: They won't change!

Anyway, when I found out Melissa was pregnant my priorities immediately changed. When I broke up with Fred that time, I finally meant it. Then I decided to quit smoking, but I still had those three packs and I planned to savor every one. I know this is disgusting for a non-smoker and I'm sorry if I am grossing you out. But when you smoke for thirty years you are attached to every pack. It's hard to think about not having the crutch. Yes, I hated it. I hated the smell. I had not smoked in my house forever. I hated the smell on my clothes, and I constantly sprayed them with Lysol. I knew it was terrible for my health and a total waste of money. I had every reason to quit and no reason not to; still it was hard, so you can understand my confusion and panic when I went to get a new pack and saw there were only two! Two? No, I know there were three. What in the world could have happened to the third pack?

I went out to the backyard, where Tyler was hanging out with his friends. They were in high school at the time. I knew Tyler didn't smoke, but I called him into the house and asked what he knew about my cigarettes.

"I know I had three packs and now there are two. Who's been in the house?"

"Well, just Joseph," he told me. Joseph was a great friend we'd known for years.

"Well, where is he? Go get him. I'm gonna kill him."

"Mom, don't embarrass him. Besides, he already left; he went home."

"I'm going to his house then. I can't believe that he would steal from me!"

Worse yet, I thought as I grabbed my keys and headed for the door, the little brat had stolen one of the last packs I would ever smoke! But Tyler easily held me back. He was bigger, taller and much stronger than I was; he had been for years.

"Mom, calm down. Why are you so mad? It's just a pack of cigarettes. I'll pay you back if you want me to."

And then I smelled it – cigarettes, on Tyler's breath!

I sniffed. There was no mistaking it, and it was definitely on him, not just his clothes. I also knew it wasn't second- hand smoke. I had to face the heart-breaking and shocking truth.

"Tyler! You smoke? You are an athlete, you are so healthy, so smart. Why would you do this? It is so stupid. You know almost every smoker wants to quit and you've decided to start."

He assured me he had just started and would quit immediately. But what else would he say?

We went outside and got the cigarettes. I took the rest of that pack, as well as the last two I had in the house and tore them up and threw them out. I have never smoked another cigarette since. I quit Fred and cigarettes within twenty-four hours, and I even quit drinking Pepsi (another addiction) that day too. What the heck, I was on a roll! Tyler taking on my bad habit had rocked me to my core.

Oh, and by the way, I "accidently" quit drinking alcohol that day too. I used to go out a few times a month with the girls, have a few drinks and sing karaoke. I knew if I had a few drinks I would want a cigarette, so I didn't go out for years. Yes, something like that – two or three years. When I finally went to a bar again, the place was so full of smoke I got a headache and a terrible hangover from the one drink I had. It was awful, and cured me of the desire to drink or smoke ever again. That's why I laugh and say "I accidently quit drinking."

Like all ex-smokers, I knew the struggle of giving up my beloved cigarettes, and it is real! And, like many, I also wound up replacing those cigarettes with food. As time went by, I could see what I was doing. I knew it, I saw it and I did it anyway. Why did I let that happen? I still remember. I made a choice. I remember thinking, *I am addicted to cigarettes; I am not addicted to food. If I get bad eating habits, I will be able to handle that. I will just quit eating candy and junk and go back to my regular way of eating.* I gotta tell ya, it's not that easy to lose weight, even after you purposely gain it. I figured if I went back to chicken Caesar salad and meat and vegies. I'd drop all the weight later. Instead, I had created a new struggle.

Growing on Purpose

My point in sharing all these struggles is that in going through them, I was getting stronger and stronger. In allowing myself to "lose" my addictions – to cigarettes, soda, Fred, and junk food, I had gained something much more valuable: confidence that I could overcome any obstacle, internal and external.

After the day I broke up with Fred, I spent ten years alone. Not a single date. I kept my head down and worked on me. I decided to figure out who I was. Yes, even after all the years, even after raising great kids and running businesses and owning homes, I still had no idea who I really was or what I wanted. My parents' plan for me was shot to hell and there was no going back. Marrying again and counting on someone else to take care of us was not an option. I just prayed that God would guide me. I had love of friends and family and that was all I've ever really needed.

Looking at myself, admitting where I'd started and considering how far I'd come, was eye- opening. I had spent my entire life to that point denying my roots. Always pretending to be something or someone I wasn't. My official story was that of a happy and healthy childhood, with no lack, no beatings, no poverty and shame. Now, though I still didn't tell too many people, I at least acknowledged it to myself. I stopped lying about the truth and worked through it, and that gave me strength. Seeing how far I had come gave me courage to take another step and another after that.

How did I do this? Like I mentioned earlier, I woke up early every morning to plan the day. I walked every morning. I did my daily crossword and had a notebook full of to-do lists. Never a dull moment. I made plans, and I accomplished them. There was no one to blame and no more excuses. Day by day, I was becoming me!

Have to, want to, should do – this was how I prioritized my day, my lists, my life. My kids had lists and notes from me too. They hated it. But this was how I got things done and it still is today. Take time for you in the first part of the day, before the world wakes up and the rollercoaster begins. I created this lifelong habit out of sheer necessity, because "early" was the only time I had to myself. My morning time has evolved, but it is still my favorite time of day. It's my time with God, and we are perfectly connected. You can plan an excellent life, in the quiet, alone with your thoughts.

I began to take pride in myself for my accomplishments, and to let all the hurt go. I decided to forgive and forget. I had lots of work to do, but I began to do it.

I'd been told by my parents not to expect too much, to be content with what I had. They convinced me and my siblings that we weren't worthy of more. This had contributed to the low self-esteem I had struggled with my entire life. But somewhere deep inside I had always known I could have, do, and be more, and now that I had some confidence I allowed it to lead the charge. Believe me, I wasn't a pillar of society, living at the top of the hill, but I lived in a descent neighborhood. My kids had ten times more than I ever asked for, which was one of – if not the biggest – benchmarks for success. I had no high-class friends, but they were no longer a n'er-do- wells either, and neither was I. I worked hard, I planned, I had many wonderful friends that loved me and helped me. I began to dream big dreams and take risks and then work my ass off to not lose it all. I did that over and over; that is how I got to where I was. If I couldn't get over the wall this way, I'd try that way. Every time I fell, I got up – every single time! That's the important part. I believed in me and went against my parents' programming.

Please don't misunderstand me, I am happy with my parents. I love my parents. I respect my parents. Things weren't perfect, but they loved us. I never had to go to therapy to get over a painful childhood. I am not resentful. They wanted what they thought was best for us. They wanted us to play it safe. They just didn't know any better. They were stuck. Stuck in lack, stuck in "not enough to go around," stuck in "money doesn't grow on trees." They tried to talk me out of every venture, every house and every business I ever started. I would show them my plans – what it would cost to buy, how much for repairs, how long it will take, and what it would be worth when I finished. I tried to show them the value, but all they ever saw was the risk.

"Ah Peg, what if the repairs cost more?" – I'll do more of the work.

"What happens if the market drops?" – Then I guess we'll live with it until it comes back up.

"Why can't you just rent a chair instead of owning a salon?"

It went on and on – all versions of the same things I'd heard growing up.

Remember, Mom? The rich get richer. Remember, it takes money to make money?

You may wonder why I kept looking for them for the go ahead. It was because I had no one else. I had no mentors, no friends who were entrepreneurs, nobody going ahead of me to show me how. Never.

They loved me, but they wanted a simple life for me. Get married, take care of your kids, home and husband. Be content with what you have. But, oh my gosh, I was not content. I wanted more. I got addicted to dreaming and achieving. I loved it and it was amazing. It still is.

Now, I *had* become content with one thing: being single. I was enjoying simply being who I had become. I had worked really hard, and I wasn't even close to being done. I still wanted a career. Not just a job, but something special.

I went back to school and graduated with a Bachelor of Arts when I was forty-five years old. Yep, that same girl who had dropped out of high school at age fifteen graduated *summa cum laude* from university thirty years later. Remember my mom told me I'd never go to college? Dad had told me, "Sorry, Sweetie, people like us don't go to college. There is just no money." Well, this girl did! While I was single, in college and raising the kids, I built a home, bought and sold houses for a profit, became a travel agent and a landlord.

Graduating from college gave my confidence a huge boost. I wasn't sure what to do next, but I knew I could accomplish anything I set my mind to. My mom said I was successful "by guess and by golly." I am not exactly sure what it means, but I could feel the truth in it. I knew it had something to do with having no guidance, just my own gut and magnificent imagination. But I also had great faith. When you know that God has your back there is nothing to fear.

By this time, I had made some money flipping those houses and I decided to get a "real" job. Did I tell you God *always* blesses me? In 2007, I decided that instead of flipping another house I would start my own insurance agency. Perfect timing, because that's when the bottom fell out of the housing market. Whew... I had dodged *that* bullet.

I purchased a small insurance agency and grew it. I was doing well enough to buy another one and merge them. Finally, I was doing it! I was a businesswoman, and a successful one too! I had always wanted to feel like this. I was making plenty of money; I traveled the world; I won awards and bonuses; I had a great staff and a beautiful office. I was asked to travel and speak and help other agents. I did it, and I loved everything about it. I also met incredible people, some of whom are my best friends today.

Then Kimberly, who was in high school, started saying things like, "Mom, I am going away to college, and I don't want to feel guilty for leaving you alone. I am not going to school here." I assured her she had nothing to worry about. I had two grandchildren now that I spent lots of time with. I had friends. And I was certainly not her responsibility. In fact, I often felt guilty for not being home with her more. I could work as much as I wanted when she left. Also, I was starting to get tired of not having a partner, of having no one to share the wins with. Of course, my friends and family were happy for me, but that's not the same.

I Always Thought That I'd See You Again

I will never forget the day Jody came back into the picture. I was sitting in church and my phone vibrated. When I looked down and saw it was a text from him, I nearly gasped out loud.

He'd sent a picture of my family's house in New York, along with the words: *Are you coming back any time soon? I've been waiting for you for thirty-five years.*

I typed as fast as my fingers would go. *Where are you? Are you in Garnerville?*

Two seconds later, my phone vibrated again.

Yes, I am here working on my daughter's house in Stoney Point.

Really? How long are you staying?

A week or two, I don't know yet. I haven't been here for a few years so I'm catching up.

My mind was racing. How could this be? I was going to be there on Friday. Finally, the stars were aligning.

I could almost imagine the shock on Jody's face when he wrote back, *This Friday?*

Yes, my son Tyler and I are going for my aunt's sixtieth anniversary of being a nun. I am staying in Stoney Point. I will call you after church.

I was overcome with emotion as the lyrics to our song, James Taylor's "Fire and Rain," flooded my mind. Could it be that after all these years, after all this bad timing, that I was actually going to see him in five days?

By that time I thought he'd given up on me. I'd not heard from him for so long.

He had called me one time when I got back from vacation with Fred – it had been a terrible trip. I was just putting my suitcase in the car when the phone rang. I had been crying. It was the worst possible time for him to call.

"I was just thinking that you are still my girl," he joked, "because you never actually broke up with me." I could hear the laughter in his voice. I could picture his face. But in that moment, instead of feeling joy or even sadness, I was filled with anger, and I did something I never did. I lashed out at him.

I told him to leave me alone. I let him know I didn't trust him. I told him I knew he cheated on me with Irene Peterson as soon as I left New York all those years ago.

Shortly after that phone call, I received a card from him. On the front Ziggy was holding a flower that flopped over, along with the words, "I'm sorry." On the inside, he had written, "Hi, I guess that was really bad timing. I hope you get to feeling better." He included both his address and his mom's, along with his phone number in case I wanted to contact him. I put the card back in its yellow envelope, then tucked it away on the second shelf of my built-in cabinet on the right-hand side. Then one day, when I was ready to contact Jody, I went to get it and found it had disappeared. I assume Fred took it, but I'll never know.

Another six years – maybe longer – went by before he found me again. I was so happy to hear from him, but he wasn't free and we didn't keep in touch. And now this! For the first time, we were both single and I was considering love again, and there he was. God always knows what He's doing. Perfect timing at last.

Then my mind – and the fear – got in the way. As our reunion grew closer, I sent him a text. *I like my life the way it is. I don't think I should see you. It will complicate things. I am scared.*

I was busy running a successful agency. I loved the time with my family, my granddaughter spent the night a lot. I had a pretty great life, and I didn't want to mess it up.

Jody convinced me to stick with the plan. I'd call when I got to town and he'd come over to talk. A few days later, we were all at my cousin's house just a few miles from his daughter, and there he was.

Is it possible to fall in love at first sight with the same person *twice*?

YES, absolutely, yes.

The truth is, the second I saw him it all flooded back. I already loved him; I still loved him. He still had the boyish grin I remembered. We both smiled a comfortable, honest smile and fell into each other's arms. I melted; I was immediately enveloped in love and comfort; He felt like "Home"; he felt like "At Last."

We stayed in the front yard for hours. My cousins would come out and say, "C'mon Peg, don't you want to come in?" but I knew they'd all be at my aunt's party the next day; I could see them then. Truth is, I didn't want to share him with the thirty-plus family members inside. I had waited decades for this, and I was enjoying every single second of it. We talked until everyone left, then Tyler and I went home, but not before Jody and I made a plan to meet the next morning.

When he came over at eight a.m. to pick me up we both admitted that we hadn't slept a wink. It was crazy. We picked up my rental car, then we went for bacon, egg, and cheese sandwiches on hard rolls. They are my favorite – I get one every trip – but that time I was too excited to eat. Saturday night I went to the party, then Sunday we had breakfast together again and spent the afternoon driving around, showing Tyler our teenage stomping grounds.

The following day, Tyler and I went to New York City for a week's vacation, and Jody headed back home to South Carolina, where he lived alone. We talked and texted every day. We'd go back and forth about how to make this work, but neither of us was sure we wanted to dive in. After all, we lived across the country from each other. I couldn't possibly give up my agency, which meant he would have to give up his life. At one point, we quit talking for about four to six weeks, but when we spoke again, it was settled. He would visit for a week or two and we'd make a decision. He came out the first of January, then he went home, packed his stuff, and came right back. We were so happy! We loved being together. He was still funny and smart and kind, and he immediately fit right in with my family and my friends. He loved them all and they loved him.

We decided to move to the house in the country, but the drive back and forth to work in Portland traffic was brutal. I would leave at six-thirty a.m. and it took well over an hour; sometimes it was two hours to get home. I started leaving at five, which made it a little better – forty-five minutes, then I'd come home and cook dinner and take care of the house. Jody took beautiful care of the property – that was our agreement and it worked – but between the commute and the full days at the office I was feeling the pressure. I still wanted to win the top awards, I wanted to be a wonderful wife, an available mom, a doting gramma and a fantastic friend. I tried to go into the office less, but the staff wasn't trained for that. I tried to change that too, but I didn't know how. I realized I wasn't doing a good job at anything anymore.

Jody's grandson came to live with us. He'd been in a lot of trouble in New York, but he was a great kid and did well with us. He got good grades and was loving. I loved him, but it was more work, more responsibility. And Jody was no longer happy like he was when he first came out. I couldn't figure out why or what to do, especially since our communication was less than honest. There just wasn't enough time in the day for me to do all that I needed to do, and I was beginning to buckle under the stress.

Finally, seeing no other way out, I sold the agency. It was my choice, but it crushed me. The agency was my pride and joy, a part of me. I had built it up from bare bones to a money-maker, the top fifteen percent of a gigantic corporation. Me, Peggy, I actually did that! I loved it so much, but in the end I decided I loved my relationship more.

Unfortunately, selling the agency still didn't change things between us. At first it seemed like it would. I had less stress and I could hardly wait for our new life together. I was so excited to see what we'd do together. That first summer, we traveled the country and had lots of adventures. For the first time in my life, I was actually feeling content.

Yet Jody still wasn't happy. He always complained that it was not *our* life, but my life that he had joined. It didn't help that he hated the cold Oregon winters. Always seeking resolution to conflict, I came up with a plan. We bought a place at a fifty-five and older complex in Arizona. We made all new friends and started a new life together. It didn't help. He still wasn't happy.

I was purposefully looking to expand my life; I was always open to the next thing. Even when I sold the business, I never thought for a second that I was done working. I just hoped we'd find something to do together. But Jody didn't want to start a business, or work on our non-profit. Yes, we had started a non-profit helping people up-level their lives a few years before. I told him that I was up for anything, that working toward a common goal would be excellent for our relationship.

Jody had always had a good sense of humor. Now, he laughingly said, "I am not only tired; I am *re*tired. It sounded funny when he said it, but in truth it really wasn't. I couldn't get him interested in anything.

When I learned of an agency for sale, Jody did say he would be a full partner, with each of us managing the office half the time. This would leave me time to work on other things I wanted to do. Plus, the agency was a good deal and a new challenge. The staff there knew that I would not always be in the office and they were used to running things. It seemed like a perfect fit. It wasn't. I sold it within a year because the clients were mainly Spanish-speaking and I never knew what anyone was talking about. I was a hundred percent responsible for everything said and done and I had no idea what was going on. There I was, a control freak who was completely out of control! It worked out perfectly, though, because I had the opportunity to mentor the young woman who had been there for years. She bought the agency from me and became a successful entrepreneur. God's plan.

When I purchased the agency, I also renewed my commitment to working on me. Even after all the work I had already done, I was stressed and unfulfilled. Discontent. I decided to engage a life coach, and that's when I met with Bill Cortright. He had created a program called Stress Mastery and did Shift Coaching. My sister had worked with him and it changed her life; in fact, she had begged me to meet him when I still had the other agency but I would never take the time. Now things were going to be different. I decided to invest in myself. A month or two after taking over the Arizona agency I started the coaching. It was amazing to learn that you have to care for yourself in all areas of your life: career, finance, relationships, health and personal development – not in any particular order. They are all essential if you are going to live a fulfilled life. Yet, as I was growing personally, Jody was retreating even more. I wanted us to work on ourselves individually and together, but he refused. It broke my heart that we were growing apart, but I couldn't go backward, only forward.

Relationships are so difficult when you have no common goals or desires. I started to realize I was fighting a losing battle; it was wearing me down. Have you known people who try to find happiness outside of themselves? He always needed something else, something more. "If it weren't for the cold winters, I'd be happy," he'd say... only he wasn't. Then it was, "If I had a new truck... a vacation with the kids... a new motorcycle or a visit with my cousins in Vegas..." It was never-ending, and these things did make him happy, it was only fleeting. He didn't understand that true happiness, true peace, only come from within.

I didn't want us to fail, I loved him still, but I was out of tools and out of ideas. I'd given all I had: compassion, forgiveness, love, kindness and care. I sought out counsel on my own; we went to counseling together, but nothing helped. One day he told me it would take much more than coffee in bed each morning, a nice clean house, and food on the table to be a good wife to him. Well, that was the eye-opener... and a real kick in the face. I had no idea he looked at me and our relationship that way. Believe me, I was a hell of a lot more than that to him, but for whatever reason he couldn't see it.

After that remark there was no going back. I had to admit defeat. I had to admit to him and myself that I could never make him happy. Lord knows I had exhausted myself trying, and all it had done was make both of us resentful. We decided to part ways as friends, and he later got back with an old girlfriend. I made peace with our breakup and wish him only love, happiness and contentment. Jody truly is a wonderful man, and I will never be sorry for our time together. He will be in my heart forever and a day.

Part Two

Who I Was Born to BE

Chapter Eight

THE NEXT ACT

There are two sides to me. Honestly, I think there are two sides to all of us. My whole life I have felt like I have an angel on one shoulder and a devil on the other. I can hear them both loud and clear – usually competing for my mind, for my will, maybe for my very soul. Do you know what I'm talking about? I bet you have them too, even if you have not yet noticed it.

I think the angel on the one shoulder is me – the Real Me, the me I want to be. The bad me on the other shoulder – that's the one I shouldn't listen to. I've always felt like she is the ego, and she's usually a jerk. You know the saying, "The devil made me, do it"? I think that the ego mind causes most of our trouble, always trying to get us to be selfish, defensive, sometimes even mean. The trouble she causes for me is constant. One minute she's on my side, saying, "Go ahead, just have a cookie. You've worked so hard at the gym. You deserve it." Then, as soon as I've enjoyed that cookie it's, "OMG I can't believe you just ate that. You worked so hard all week and then blew it! You have no will power."

Sometimes she shows up in other ways, like: "You need to stick up for yourself, next time – have some self-respect!" The next minute it's: "Boy, you really blew it! Should have kept your mouth shut."

All that negative self-talk really messes with us and the way we see ourselves.

How do you know who you are born to be when you have this constant conflict inside of you? I can use this book for example. I had the idea, this spark, to write it at least thirty years ago. Yes, it's that old! But anytime I ever wanted to start I made up a million excuses. "I was too busy"; "I'm not a writer"; "I don't have a good enough vocabulary." And the number one reason to procrastinate: "You will just make a fool of yourself. Nobody cares what you have to say, Peggy! Do you get that? Nobody cares!"

Has this happened to you? What ideas have you let go of? What unfulfilled desires do you have in your heart? Do you leave dreams unfulfilled and goals untried because you talked yourself out of them? Does it make you feel better to know that you're not alone? It happens to all of us.

Do you find comfort in the fact that you are not crazy, even though you've probably spent countless hours, years even, arguing with yourself? And how can you argue with your Self? Aren't we just one mind? Perhaps, but we do it anyway.

For a long time I thought I was nuts with this internal back and forth. I mean, who in the world was I really fighting? Who was the real me? Then I learned that everybody has this pest known as the ego. I named mine. You should too. It makes it easier to notice.

I call her Lucy, and to be honest, I hate to even capitalize the name, for fear of giving her more power than she already has. I have to remind myself, *I am not the voice in my head.*

It's important that we acknowledge the ego's existence and name that little brat so we can become aware of who he/she is, and stop confusing him/her with who we really are. Once you give it a name – and the sooner the better – you will then start to notice who is talking, and who you're listening to. Lucy is a bossy little "B"; she fills me with fear. She doesn't ever want me to change.

Look at it this way, how are we supposed to know who we are born to be if we don't know which one we are? Again, I know it sounds crazy but after you name your ego and pay attention to what it says, you will be able to distinguish between the two and concentrate on developing the real you – the you, you were born to be.

Whew... I hope you're still with me.

I had no idea who I was for most of my life! How could I know who I was born to be when I always allowed my ideas to be squashed? I did follow through on some – usually just the smaller ones. I allowed myself to step out of my comfort zone just a bit. I allowed myself to try a few things.

Though I worked hard to make a life for myself, it was about survival. I didn't allow myself to dream big dreams. I never saw my true value. For years, I sabotaged my own future. I squashed my own dreams. I talked myself out of ideas, including some really great ones.

I was always willing to listen to "Lucy," though of course at the time I didn't know it was "her." She's the one who said, "You can't go to college"; "You can't make a good salary"; "You will never buy a house"; "Be thankful for what you have"; "Why can't you be content?"; and "Who do you think you are, anyway?" Lucy would beat me down and tell me I couldn't do it, whatever *it* was. She is relentless, badgering me until I gave up and then chastise me for not trying hard enough. So many times, I gave up on myself without even giving myself a chance. I quit before even giving most things a try. What a waste of time, what a waste of life. I am hoping that you will not do this to yourself, not for another day.

Chapter Nine

BUILDING CONFIDENCE

*E*ach of us have defining moments in life – opportunities for us to either go forward or fall back. For me, one of those moments was when Mark left me. I could have curled up in a ball, but instead I chose to move forward and stop believing the lies. Remember I said that my real life began at age twenty-seven? Well, something came alive in me when he proclaimed, "I don't think I will get anywhere as long as I'm with you." I am truly grateful to him for saying that to me. It changed my life. It gave me a reason to propel myself to bigger and better things. At first, I was just trying to prove something to him, but then it was to prove it to myself. I have never stopped since.

I hope you too will come to the realization that proving your worth to yourself is much more rewarding than trying to prove it to anyone else. The same thing happened when Jody let me know he needed more to consider me a "good wife." Has someone said something like this to you? If so, enough. You are the one that matters. You are *always* the one that matters!

Discouraged

When I was twelve and in the sixth grade, I wrote a song. I wrote the lyrics and asked my dad to play it on the guitar. I'm pretty sure that he just couldn't catch the melody I wanted for my song, because as he often told me, "I can't carry a tune in a bucket." Don't be too hard on the man; he's not the only one who has ever told me that. I do love to sing, though, and I do it loud and proud, though usually it's in the car when nobody can hear me!

My point is, that was my one and only attempt at songwriting. You know why? Because my dad told me, "That song has already been written." He thought it sounded like "Blowin' in The Wind" by Bob Dylan. But no, it did not – at least, not in my imagination! He just couldn't pick up the tune I was looking for and I certainly couldn't carry it. We probably didn't try for more than two or three minutes. It's relevant to point out that Dad loved music. We all sang and danced as he played the guitar; it was a regular occurrence in our household when I was young. He taught Chris the chords and I think he in turn taught them to the younger boys. For some reason the boys were encouraged to play music, but in Dad's mind I was not a songwriter; it was more than he could hope for me to be.

Growing up they had a garage band that led to paid gigs around Portland. They were really quite good (remember, they played at my wedding to Dean?), and our whole family and all of our friends went to see them often. What would my dad have done if Chris had brought him song lyrics to play a tune for? I can only assume he would have encouraged it. Better question: what if he had applauded the creative spark I had? Unfortunately, there is no way to know, because I let him stop me in my tracks. I sang the song to my nephew Jordan a while back and he figured out how to play it. It doesn't sound anything like "Blowin' in the Wind."

How many times have you taken no for an answer? Have you let one person's opinion change your mind about something? What are the desires of your heart? Who told you that you can't? What if they are wrong?

It's Okay to be vulnerable.

I beg you to start dreaming again. Picture what you want. Be bold and have fun. Spend some time writing it all down.

Sometimes just barely enough is just not enough.

I know that it's hard to do things when you don't know how, but you have to start somewhere. You can start small if that's easier for you – just pick something you've wished you can do, then stop wishing and start doing.

With some planning and encouragement, I bet you can.

I have tried and failed at lots of stuff. I get scared and quit, or I get scared and do it anyway. Right now, I am writing this book and guess what? I am scared. Sometimes I am scared to death. I am making myself vulnerable. It's hard looking back and telling the world all about me, and admitting to the skeletons in my closet. So many things I am not proud of. So many things I wish hadn't happened. There are things my kids don't know about – I have to tell them before they read it. My friends don't know all that stuff either; I don't like to talk about it. At times, I've felt like crying between chapters, but I wrote them anyway. I realize that those "bad" things that made me who I am. All of that stuff is how I got here.

This is me, the real me. The old me would have quit by now. With each page, with every word, I am getting more and more confident. If I fail or succeed at being a fabulous author, I am being true to myself. I am doing this for me. I am doing this because I want to help you. I've known for my whole life that God put me here for a purpose. I've known for decades that my purpose is to help other people. I love helping people!

I put stuff off, procrastinate because of fear. When I don't know how, I freeze. I am so tired of letting fear stop me in my tracks. I am going for it. I am doing it afraid! I want peace. I want the peace of knowing that my dream is fulfilled. I want the peace that comes from doing your best. I don't want to look back and say "what if?" – like I have to do with that number-one hit song that was never written. I missed my chance at being a songwriter. But since you are reading this, I am a published author! I am a writer! I did it!

What are you missing out on and why are you allowing that? If you don't know, go back and read the introduction again – it's fear, and you can do it anyway!

It doesn't matter who is saying you can't; it might be you or someone else, maybe even several people. Step past that. Tell yourself, "Oh yes, I can" and then go for it. Empower yourself to take a step out of your comfort zone, which as we know, is highly *un*comfortable. I know the ego is trying to pull you back in, but I promise you, once you do it, it will become easier. There's at least one thing we can agree on: You will never make it if you don't try.

Now remember, I'm not suggesting that you dive in haphazardly. Make a plan, set your goal, and then figure out what steps you will need to take to get there. The last thing I want is for you to jump off a roof with a parachute that doesn't open because I said you can fly. I want you to PLAN on success. That said, don't get caught up in the plan. Planning too much or planning to long is another form of procrastination. Procrastination is usually caused by more fear... and that ego.

I don't want to be afraid of being my real self any longer. I am a better person than what I believed most of my life. I am better than the idea I had of myself, the one that I was given as a child. That wasn't me. That was my parents' idea of me. Society's idea of me. My brother's idea of me. Not *my* idea of me. I decided to flip the script. I get to say who I am now. And so do you.

Are you living your dream that you imagined for yourself? Or are you stuck in the cage others put you in? Change your mindset and step out of the cage. It's your comfort zone, but it's not actually all that comfortable, is it? It's not always easy, but it's worth it.

Chapter Ten

FIND YOUR WHY

I am not sure how old I was when it began, but I realized that my parents were stuck in the belief that they were destined to be poor. Thus we, as a family, were destined to be poor. I was told many times that I could not expect more than that. That was the hand I was dealt, my lot in life, Mom said. We had free lunch at school, no abundance of food at home, always wanted something we couldn't afford. The latter I think is probably normal for most kids, everybody wants more stuff. But we were taught that the mindset of not having enough was okay. It was our normal, having more bills than money, living in survival mode, and always needing something. My parents were always just trying to get by. It was enough for them; it was okay with them to live like that. I don't think they ever wished for any more than just enough. So that was all they ever had.

"It'll be slim pickins around here until payday," Mom would often say. Making it from payday to payday was enough for them. I thank God it's not enough for me.

I don't remember when I started to question that lack mentality that I was raised in. I started wondering, Why do we have to be poor? Doesn't dad have a good job? How much are the bills? Why does our electricity get shut off at least once a year for not paying the bill? Do you know when the bill is coming? Do we have to buy steak and go out for ice cream when we get paid? Why don't we buy ice-cream and cones at the store and have them three times instead of going out for ice-cream once? Can't we buy one pair of shoes at a time so you don't have to buy seven pairs at the last minute, all out of one paycheck? You already know there won't be enough money when school starts...

I wanted to understand why we had to live like this. I wanted answers. If I know me, I was hoping to solve the problem. The only answer I got was, "It's none of your business, Peggy"; "You don't understand, Peggy"; "You're a kid; You have no idea."

Admittedly, I was a kid – maybe around ten – but I was old enough to know better, old enough to see what was going on. Back in the day, it was safe to send your kids to the store and I learned the prices of things early. I could see the value of not wasting money. I'd go a few times a week for a gallon of milk, a loaf of bread, and a pack of cigarettes – those were the staples, the fill-ins. My parents went grocery shopping every two weeks, and we couldn't wait for the goodies to make it home. I am not sure why they didn't buy fourteen dinners at a time, surely, they knew how many meals there were between paydays. We'd have sweet cereal, steak, chocolate milk, cookies and candy for the first week. The second we'd scrimp, a tiny bit of meat with bread and gravy was sometimes our dinner. One pound of hamburger shared between the nine of us. It was good and I was used to it; but I did notice that if we bought more hamburger meat instead of the two steak dinners, we could make four meals with less money. Unfortunately, when we got a little older, frozen meals came out, and that's what we lived on. Convenience food, it was much more expensive than real food back then. It was easy and Mom didn't have to cook much anymore. I don't know why I noticed the money wasted on feeding the family. I guess it was because I didn't like the frozen Salisbury steak and the chicken and dumplings. My mom knew how to make a few things like beans and ham and split pea soup. Why couldn't we have that more often? I may have tried to suggest such things – I was already learning to cook – but I assume I was shut down the same way I was when I tried to get them to budget household money more carefully. It wasn't long after that, when I was about eleven or twelve years old, when I made a promise to myself that I would figure out how to make my money last.

- My kids will always have enough food. Good food and as much as they want.
- I will know how to cook lots of things and not eat instant food.
- I'm not going to have a bunch of kids if I don't make enough to support them all.
- I am not going to waste all my money on extra things and then run out before payday.
- I am going to have a budget and plan ahead for the things I know I will need.
- I will have presents for Christmas for my kids but I will not let the electricity get shut off in January.
- I will always make sure I fill my oil tank before winter comes so that we will always have heat in the house in the winter.

This was the basic checklist I had in my head at a very young age. As time went on, I internalized the idea that my lot in life was to be poor and lacking basics, yet that list became longer. Coats and shoes were very important to me. We had holes in our shoes sometimes and in the winter we tried to cover them with a piece of cardboard covered in plastic wrap. It was wet, cold and embarrassing!

I made a promise to myself. If I have to be poor, I'm going to do my best at being poor. I wanted my kids to have enough. Enough food, clothes and shoes and fun! I believed that if I could do that, I'd be a success! That was my life's goal in my adolescence. (Remember I was "destined" to be a housewife.)

Sure enough, I did okay when I went out on my own. I was only seventeen, but I was determined to live as a grownup. I made a budget right away and usually stuck to it, though admittedly not as well as I could have and not as often as I would have liked. I messed up lots of times. It was nice to spend money on things you like and want. I adjusted my budget when needed and I never had my utilities shut off and I never went hungry. But I soon realized I wanted more than that. What if I tried even harder? Could I do better?

Mom always said, "The rich get richer." Okay then, I asked, how can I get rich? I am too poor to go to college. I am too poor to meet anyone with a good job because they are "out of my league" – not that I ever met people who had their act together. According to my mother, my legs weren't even nice enough to get a secretarial job! I would just have to work hard and not waste money. I understood the cards were not in my favor. This was incredibly hard for me to accept, and yet I did sort of accept it. That was all I could see; I was programmed to make the best of your life with the little you have, and be happy with it. "You have a lot more than a lot of people," I was told. "Be grateful and content." Those were the cards I was dealt in life. I could see the problem; I just could not see the solution. I doubt I even knew there was one!

From a Mindset of Lack to Prosperity

Deciding I wanted more than barely enough brought up other questions. *Was it really a sin to want more? Why wasn't it okay to work hard and save up for stuff? Shouldn't I just try to do my best? Do I have to accept this as my life? Do I have to struggle just because we always had?* It never occurred to me to dream of being a "fancy millionaire." I never dreamed of making it too far up the ladder. I was not trying to be better than anyone else. But couldn't I at least be a person who can go on vacations? Couldn't I take my kids to Disneyland someday? Couldn't I dream of taking a cruise or going to Europe? Would it be at all possible to save up enough money to go to nursing school? I could make more money then and, who knows, maybe I could meet a doctor to marry. Couldn't I somehow make enough money for my kids to go to college? If so, how do I do that? Why did I have to be born poor? Don't I have a choice? Do I *really* have to stay this way?

Mom also believed the Bible said that "Money is the root of all evil" and she engrained that in my head. *Surely, I don't want to go to hell over money. Are rich people really going to hell? What if they are good people? What if a rich person believes in Jesus? Is he still going to hell?* ...And, in case you don't know it, the Bible doesn't actually say that.

I pondered these things for years, throughout my late teens and into my twenties. Mark didn't like to save; he liked to spend, always wanting more than what we had. Once again, there was never enough. We used credit cards and car loans to get what we wanted, so we were always broke. I hated it. I didn't want to waste all that money on interest, but I did for years. I always worked a side hustle and had cash. Things like babysitting or house-cleaning. My kids always had nice clothes and plenty of food, toys, and love. And we did have a better life than my family did growing up. Hell, I was even helping my parents financially because they still didn't get their bills paid, even after all the kids moved out. I went on my first real vacation when I was twenty-three years old. I loved it! I wanted more of this life, and I was determined to have it.

Be Bold Enough to be You!

After Mark and I broke up, I began to question the reality I was born into, and the lack mentality my parents had passed down to me. I had believed it all, until then – bought it hook, line, and sinker. Now I realized I had been willing to settle for less than my very best life, just because they told me I had to. But who were they to tell me I had to be poor? Why was I believing it?! Why did I have to be a housewife who didn't work? I was smart. I might be good at something. At that time, I didn't know what it was yet ... but I knew there must be something. I was trying to find my way out of a cave that I had lived my whole life in. This is a very scary place to be. I was still young and again, my friends also struggled; we all had nothing. I had no role models, which I think is the hardest part. All I had succeeded at so far was buying a house and a car. The American Dream. I was trying to be happy with that, but I knew there was more than just, "We're okay" and "It doesn't matter if you are happy with your job, be happy you have one." Yes, I was already doing a little better than my parents, but I still wanted more. Money in the bank, maybe, or no debt and the house paid off. At the same time, I was thinking, Why do I think I need more than everyone else I knew? They were all renting and I was buying my house. Would I lose my friends if I did somehow build a better life? Would it be worth it to lose them if I got what I wanted? What would my family say if I stepped out of that cage we were all forced into?

In the meantime, I did everything I could to make sure my kids would not have to struggle as I was. I talked to them about what we had and how I needed to spend it. I taught them to be responsible with money. I was happy knowing that my kids would even be further along than I was, and that their children would be better off still, all because of what I was teaching them now. I was breaking the cycle of the lack mentality mindset, not just for me and my siblings, but for future generations.

It's Never Too Late

Once I shed the belief that I was destined to be poor, it was gone for good. I started looking at what I had achieved, which was quite a lot! I was not yet thirty, and I had a plan to pay off the house by the time I was thirty-eight. After that, I might rent it out and buy another. It was risky and challenging, but I could SEE myself in the future. A future with money in the bank and the ability to do what I wanted. Once I saw it, I couldn't "un-see" that new vision of my destiny.

You too can step up and out of that mindset forever. Each and every step gives you a bit more confidence. Each success, no matter how small, gives you the gumption to keep going, which leads to another step and more confidence. See how it works? But you have to be willing to take the first step.

I am using money in this illustration, but that isn't the most important thing you gain. You gain knowledge and personal strength. Self-respect and confidence. You learn to value yourself. You gain wisdom and freedom to make choices for yourself. When you feel good about yourself, you have better relationships. I cannot begin to tell you what life looks like from a different perspective. You'll need to experience it for yourself.

Imagine

As I took each step, making adjustments along the way, I continued to allow myself to dream. And, over time, I realized that these same steps could work for all my goals. It doesn't matter what you want better in your life. Use your imagination. Picture where you want to be every day. Dream it, write down your goals, and figure out the steps. Be brave. Then, one by one, work the steps you need to get there. Reassess your goals often, and what you need to do to get there. You might have working in the yard, grocery shopping, going for a walk after lunch, or taking the kids to the park after work. Or you might have starting your own business at the top of your list, or going to college or getting out of debt. What do you want to do today? Write it down and do it. Keep your promise to yourself. Take small steps that lead to big goals.

Anything you procrastinate about should definitely go on this list. If you don't do it today, it goes on the top of the list tomorrow. Generally, when I am procrastinating it's because I'm afraid the outcome won't be what I want or am hoping for. Do it anyway; get it over with. It moves you to the next thing, one way or another. This is also where you write the idea you want and what you need to do to change your life. One thing at a time, day after day. It really works.

We all come from different places and I know your situation is more than likely totally different than mine. The steps you take will be different, but if you stay on course, you will be able to change your life like I did. It doesn't matter where you are today. Picture a better tomorrow and you will have it. Really.

Do you see things that you know don't make sense and accept them as the way it is, or normal? If you know it's wrong, it's wrong. Stop accepting it! Ask yourself, how could this be done better? Make that a goal on your list, and figure out, step by step, how to change that one thing, and then do it. Each win, even the small ones, will build upon each other, and build your confidence.

Don't have a budget? Write one. It doesn't matter how much or how little money you have. You are spending your money on something; don't you think you should tell your money where to go? Write it down and stick to it.

Want to go back to school? Start by going to the admissions office, see what that looks like. What does it cost? Can you get financial aid? Look at the classes, which ones would you like to take? Find out how to get there from here. You don't know what you don't know. Find out. Each step is a victory, so go for it, be proud of it, celebrate it.

Bottom line: we get to decide who we are. Nobody else. The sooner you believe that, the sooner you will get on with your life. I'm talking about your life, where the Real You lives. Your heart and soul. The one and only you that you were born to be. You are still there, inside just waiting to show the world what you're made of and who you really are. I wasn't created to be a woman without hope of an education, without dreams to live for, without respect of a husband or enough money to live a nice life. That's who they said I was, who I was programmed to be. It wasn't me. I am very grateful for that God-given inner spark that didn't allow me to accept that as my destiny. It's what gave me the determination to fight my way out of that "I can't" mindset. The next time you catch yourself saying, "I can't," be honest with yourself and admit that "you won't" - because that is your decision.

Conclusion

MY HISTORY IS NOT ME

That brings me here, to today. I am working on Peggy – just for me, the real me. I just turned sixty. That may seem old to some of you, but I know I still have a full life ahead of me. Lots of plans, dreams, and things to do – and I can't wait! I am so excited to see what God has in store for me. I am full of exuberance and excitement every day. I am finally at a place where I can see my future the way I want it.

Jody moved out and away a year ago. Sometimes it is still hard for me to believe that I have never lived alone before. I have always had someone to take care – from my parents and siblings to my partners and children. Of course, I believe you should put your kids first when they are young, and I love every minute I have with my baby grands, Riley and Aliza. But it is important to put yourself first too, and that's what I'm doing now. I am doing the work that I want to do. I don't have kids at home, no husband to cook dinner for. I don't have children in college or bills waiting to get paid. This is my time to learn and grow and be me. And to help you.

I gotta be honest, it feels pretty funny sometimes. But I know I am doing what God wants me to do. I am doing the big stuff it takes courage to do. Growing and learning and writing takes time. I have set a timeline and a schedule inside my goals. I am going for it and I am so excited! I am also scared and completely out of my comfort zone. Once again, the "what-ifs" try to stop me.

What if I fail? *Then I'll figure it out and try again, like I always do.*

What if nobody buys my book? *Then I will remember it was for me.*

What if I am a lousy coach and don't help people? *What if I help even one?*

Then again...

What if I am an amazing coach, a bestselling author, and I help tons of people by sharing my experiences – good, bad and ugly?

What if I am helping you gain confidence in yourself right now, because you're reading this book?

Over time, I have gained more courage, one step at a time. I may do it scared, but I do it anyway.

Now, I am a risk-taker. In the past I set many goals for myself, but sometimes I stayed inside the lines. Usually, I mustered the courage to step out of the mold I was placed in, but just a bit. Not this time. Now I am going all in. I am thrilled about my life. I love it. And I am totally excited for you to discover the potential inside of you too.

I know there is always something in the way, something to stop us from pursuing our greatest desires. I know many of our dreams seem too big, too bold, but they aren't. That's just your fear! There is usually a way around the obstacles if you are willing to invest in yourself. Those dreams in your heart are there for a reason. No one can achieve them but you. Don't give up on yourself, you are too important.

You don't have to go it alone. Find someone you trust to talk to about your goals. Maybe it's a mentor or a life coach; maybe it's a friend or family member. Community colleges have free academic counseling. Find someone on social media or someone at work. There is someone somewhere that you admire. Someone who is walking in the direction of their dreams. Someone who's killing it. It might be someone you meet in person, or an author whose book you read, or a podcast host you listen to. What are they doing? Modify it, and do that. Just get busy.

I am finally doing what I am telling you to do. Dream your dreams and set your course. During this process of becoming an author I searched online for "how to write a book." I have talked to younger people about how to use Instagram. I am learning how to market myself on social media. I look at websites and listen to public speakers – I do anything I can to educate myself. Honestly, I don't know what I am doing, but I am figuring it out. I have to. Nobody else can do it for me. We all have a different road to take. Find yours.

Integrity to Self

I have made countless promises to other people over the years, and I kept every one of them, but I haven't always done the same for myself. I would get too busy or didn't feel like it or for whatever reason I decided to procrastinate, or, worse yet, quit. I do my best to not do that anymore. Life is just too short. If I make a promise to myself, I keep it. Writing this book is one example.

If you have done the same thing, the time is now to start keeping those promises. It is my hope that you will make your dreams, your goals, and yourself a priority. It's okay to be selfish sometimes. You have time for everyone else in your day, so make time for you – even if it's just one hour a day. Skip a tv show or get up an hour earlier – whatever you need to do to find some time. Start somewhere. You are worth it. Would you believe that procrastination is just fear in a different package? It is. So, stop it.

I Live in Peace

The decision to coach with Bill Cortright changed my entire life, because it changed my beliefs. He taught me how to set down the heavy load I had been carrying all my life. He helped me to see that I get to choose the person I want to be. What I think, what I do. I get to be as successful as I decide to be. I get to be as kind, as daring, as loving as I choose. It's my choice and it's all on me. I wish I had made myself a priority sooner. I guess it may be God's timing, but I see it clearly now. What an awakening.

What a feeling of peace I have now! I see the tremendous amount of unnecessary stress I once placed on myself. I worried about things that didn't matter, things I could do nothing to change. I was used to feeling unsettled, looking for something, for someone, outside myself. I wanted everyone to be happy and tried to be the person that they thought I should be or wanted me to be. I finally realize that everything that has happened to me, good and bad, every success or failure, should be celebrated. It has led me to where I am – and who I am – today.

These days, I continue to live with the end in mind; I will finish my race strong. I know full well that there will be many twists and turns on the way to achieving my goals. I know I will have failures and be disappointed in myself. I will brush off my knees and my pride, and then I will get back up. Others will try to discourage me, either because they are afraid for me or because they are afraid of who I am becoming. "What if you fall on your butt?" they'll say. My answer: "I will get back up. It's what I do. It's what I have done a hundred times before.

It has taken me so long to get to this place. I wasted years not being truly happy when I surely could have been. I have spent my life just "getting by" emotionally. I am praying that you don't do that, but if you already have, don't judge yourself, just know there is a better way. Just get to it and start living your life now. I have done much better than I ever thought possible.

I never considered myself to be someone working on personal development. I was just trying to survive, and in fact my determination has been ninety percent desperation. Many times, I did accomplish what I set out to do. Sometimes it worked out better than I expected, but I never experienced peace. I didn't even think it was possible, and spent many sleepless nights because I had a problem and did not know how to solve it. I have taken things out on my kids because I had pent-up aggravation and excessive negative energy and didn't know where to go with it. I am not proud of it, but it's true. I am so sorry for all that, and they know it. I have apologized to each of them individually and asked for forgiveness, and I hope they value the commitment I have made to be a great mom in their adult lives. I am looking for peace for all of us now. Better late than never, I say.

One of the affirmations I say all day long is "I live in peace." Guys, it works! I do live in peace! I am as busy as I have ever been and I am at peace all day, every day. I have a busy schedule, and I love it. I am not stressed out because of the pressure. I don't want to slow down or quit, not for a long time. Recently my sister Jenny said, "If you ever call and tell me that you are retiring, I will take that to mean, 'My life is over, please come now and shoot me; get me out of my misery.'" We both laughed at the thought of me sitting around all day with no purpose or plan. She is the same way.

So here I am starting my life over, but it is different this time, because *I* am different. There is no fear, there is no force. I make my plans every day, but now, I take things as they come. I am flexible. When fear creeps in, I am now able to let it go and move forward without spending a week asking others what they think I should do.

Be ready to be flexible. Things will always happen that take us a bit sideways on the path, usually when we least expect it. This means we will always have stress; it is part of being human and living on this earth. But I have learned to manage my stress so it goes as quickly as it comes. I remind myself that life is happening for me, not to me. I have learned from my mistakes. I have learned to trust that when something goes awry, I can say "Thank you, I will need this lesson down the road, I just know it!"

It is my hope that I will inspire many people to change for the better. To learn and be willing to let go of the hurt. To let go of the heartache that they've carried with them their whole lives. To let go of other people's expectation of who they are supposed to be. To finally be the authors of their own lives, to be who they choose to be. It is an amazing and wonderful space to be in.

That said, it also important to acknowledge your foundation, including the supportive people you have in your life. My family is the best, and I couldn't ask for more support from them. My siblings love me unconditionally. They support me in all I do. They always have my back. They believe in me without question. It's funny that they just expect that I will be successful, they don't see me as vulnerable to defeat, which of course, I am. They no longer ask, "Are you sure you should try that?' They know it will work out.

My three children are also incredible people – smart, strong, hardworking, full of integrity and charm. They are funny, and usually the life of the party, easily fitting in wherever they go. I am happy that the skills they learned growing up have helped them in their adult lives. They are able to roll with the punches and can see the bright side of every situation. I cannot imagine what my life would have been without them, but "empty" would be my guess, because they are absolutely everything that is important to me.

It always amazes me how different they all are, despite being raised in the same house by the same person, yet they are all grounded by family.

Melissa, an insurance agent, is a beautiful, smart, and independent woman. She is also the mother of my two beautiful grandkids, Riley and Aliza Grace. Melissa loves to hang out with friends and family, and enjoys travel almost as much as she enjoys being at home and taking care of her plants. She is a fabulous person and the apple of my eye. She just told me a few days ago that she loves the new me. That alone has made my time and investment worth it.

While Melissa loves stability, sameness (probably because we had to move around so many times when she was young), the other two are more like me – willing to pick up and go if they spy what could be an exciting or profitable venture on the horizon.

My boy Ty moved to Iowa in search of a better life than he could find in Portland's inner city. He is extremely intelligent and a very hard worker. He has a beautiful girlfriend he intends to marry, and I look forward to several grandchildren in the coming years. He supports all I do and is always there to give me strength and encouragement.

Kimberly, my little love bug, went away to college, just as she had always intended. She is an executive assistant at a wonderful company and makes a great living. She keeps her eye on the prize and will continue to be promoted. She really has turned into a beautiful woman, a true friend and always my biggest fan.

I have such a wonderful life. I am ever so grateful for my friends and my family who have stuck by me through thick and thin. Believe me, these people have had to get their hands dirty, literally, when I got in over my head with houses I was flipping or living in... or things I started and couldn't figure out how to finish. They also came to me no matter what job I did. It was always, "Get your haircut from me"; "Let me sell your house"; "Plan a trip through my travel agency"; and "Let me quote your insurance." Or, "Can you come real quick, I took down a load bearing wall?"; "Could you please help me finish this tile job, lay these floors with me, or help me paint my twenty-six-hundred-foot house, please?"; "Do you know how to build a deck or put in a sprinkler system?" Or, one of the most common ones: "Oh, I am moving again, can you help me?"

Wow, writing it out makes me look like a big pain... now I feel even more blessed that they've stuck with me! Just so you know, I will do anything for my friends and family too. I love to help people and will go out of my way to do so, as long as they're willing to learn and grow. I'm happy to give a hand up, but not always a hand-out... and I wouldn't have it any other way.

While support is important, it really doesn't matter what anyone else thinks of your goals. They are yours; they are for you. You are the one who has to step out and do it. You are the only one who will regret it if you don't. I have lost many people in my life simply because I couldn't drag them along. There will always be people who try to pull you back; they can't help it. They want you to stay the same, and who you are becoming – that better version of you – makes them uncomfortable. The point is, you cannot let that stop you.

I've had a million "reasons" over the years for not doing things I wanted to do – and honestly, they were usually valid ones. I also told myself at least a million times, "Yes, it's scary, but do it anyway." Guys, you will gain momentum when you do that. When you fall and get back up you realize you aren't dead, you aren't defeated. Just get back up and try again. Learning to fall, learning to fail is actually a very good thing. If you can't push past the fear and go for it, how will you ever learn how strong you really are? We all have a great potential. We are all made to do great things. You are here on purpose, for a purpose. Life is here for you. Are you really going to allow yourself to sit on the couch and watch life pass you by? Or are you going to finally become the person you were always meant to be?

Reach out to me, I am here to help you:

Website: PeggyRomero.com

Instagram: https://instagram.com/peggywithpurpose

Facebook: https://facebook.com/PeggyWithPurpose/

Podcast: LivingRightWithBillCortright (I am there on Saturdays.)

Coaching: PeggyRomero.com

ABOUT THE AUTHOR

Peggy Romero is a successful entrepreneur, motivational speaker, and certified life coach with a mission to help others to dream big and live up to their true potential. She is also the co-founder of Dream, a non-profit dedicated to assisting women as they learn to discover and honor their authentic selves, and holds workshops on financial empowerment.

Growing up, Peggy endured physical abuse, emotional trauma and poverty while caring for her six siblings. Married and pregnant at age eighteen, she found herself struggling to keep her family together in the face of her husband's alcoholism. Peggy believes her life began at age twenty-seven, when her first marriage ended. Vowing to provide a better life for her children, she learned to face her fears and shed the lack mindset that had plagued her throughout her life. Mapping out her goals and the steps needed to achieve them, she went on to own two beauty salons, a travel agency, and insurance agencies under the Allstate umbrella, winning several awards for her work in that industry.

Despite her many successes, however, Peggy realized she was still operating from a place of stress and worry. A major turning point came when she began working with leading stress management expert Bill Cortright, eventually becoming certified as a Stress Mastery Shift Coach. She also appears regularly on Bill's podcast, *Living Right with Bill Cortright.*

When she is not working, Peggy enjoys decorating, traveling, cooking and, most of all, spending time with her siblings, children and grandchildren, and many friends.

ACKNOWLEDGMENTS

I am truly blessed with the best people ever – wonderful friends, a big family who loves me, and a church family that has supported me through thick and thin for over twenty-five years, and Bill Cortright, who has changed my entire life.

But I have to say that above all I have had one true and constant friend in my life, and that is Shelly. No matter what I do she is always there, believing in me, nudging me when I need it to keep moving along and calling me out on my crap when it's called for. When I fall, she helps me up. When I cry, she dries my tears. When I am about to make the same mistake again, she gently reminds me that it may not work out the way I want it to. My life would not have been the same without her constant love, encouragement, and support. Words cannot express the gratitude I have for her. Thank you, Shelly!

www.ingramcontent.com/pod-product-compliance
Lightning Source LLC
Chambersburg PA
CBHW070700130626
46553CB00005B/1778